Asian Tigers for Christ

THE REVD DR MICHAEL GREEN is Adviser in Evangelism to the Archbishops of Canterbury and York, and Senior Research Fellow at Wycliffe Hall, Oxford.

Asian Tigers for Christ

The Dynamic Growth of the Church in South East Asia

MICHAEL GREEN

First published in Great Britain in 2001
Society for Promoting Christian Knowledge
Holy Trinity Church
Marylebone Road
London NW1 4DU

ACKNOWLEDGEMENTS
Unless otherwise stated, biblical quotations are from
The New Revised Standard Version of the Bible © 1989, 1995.

British Library Cataloguing-in-Publication Data
A catalogue record for this book is available from
the British Library

ISBN 0-281-05369-3

Typeset by Pioneer Associates, Perthshire
Printed in Great Britain by
Omnia Books, Glasgow

Contents

*A modest tribute to the
archbishop and bishops of the
Province of South East Asia*

Foreword

The Most Revd Datuk Yong Ping Chung,
Archbishop of the Province of the Anglican Church
in South East Asia

———•———

Not by might nor by power, but by My Spirit (Zechariah 4.6)

With great joy, deep gratitude and mighty praise and
thanksgiving to God we celebrate the publication of this
book on our Province by our good friend Canon Michael
Green. *Asian Tigers for Christ* becomes even more significant
and challenging when it is read in the context of the Asian
Tigers of contemporary Asia. The mighty roar of the Asian
Tigers was struck down almost overnight. Even with all their
political will, military power and human strength, these Asian
Tigers were not able to combat the onslaught of the collapse
of the Asian economy. In the twinkling of an eye the economic bubble was burst. The whole of Asia slumped back
into its dark ages. Suffering, despair, poverty, unrest, disorder
and bloodshed clawed the land. The media have effectively
brought all these to the attention of the world.

Michael Green, who has visited us as frequently as possible
and ministered side by side with us for many years, especially
in outreach and evangelism in our local scene, has become a
personal friend. With his keen spiritual eye and personal in-
depth understanding of many of us, he saw the emergence of
a profound spiritual reality in our land. He applied his special
gift of writing and skilfully captured the normal day-to-day
manifestation of the Holy Spirit in the life and ministry of
very ordinary clergy, pastors and lay people of our church.
Asian Tigers for Christ tells genuine, exciting stories of
our people empowered by the Holy Spirit to minister for
the glory of God and advancement of God's kingdom in

our land. We are a young church. Thus most of the people in this story are still alive in ministry with us. Revival and renewal are still very much part of our daily happening.

We see clearly the underlying conditions for such an explosive growth in the early Church. The disciples were united in spirit and in truth. They submitted themselves to the authority of the Scripture of their day and the teaching of the apostles received from the Lord Jesus. They were deep in prayer, active in ministry, vibrant in worship and bold in declaring that Jesus died and rose again as the Lord and God of their life. They took the Great Commission seriously. Every situation was used as an opportunity to lift Jesus high for the glory of God. We read the account of the Acts of the Apostles with deep conviction and thanksgiving.

We pray that we will faithfully model our church after the spirit of the early Church, so that 'The Lord will add to our number daily those who are being saved' (cf. Acts 2.47).

Asian Tigers for Christ is Michael Green's deep desire and fervent prayer for our church in Asia. It is his gracious way to affirm and to encourage us. We are grateful to Michael for his constant and solemn reminder of our unfinished task and urgent mission for the Lord. In the Province of South East Asia, we have nine nations and 400 million souls to reach. At times, we feel so powerless. Thus, the word of God through the prophet Zechariah is a real comfort and challenge for us:

Not by might, nor by power, but by MY SPIRIT

I know Michael Green's heart's desire and fervent prayer is also a timely and urgent reminder for all churches today. We all need to rise up and be counted. We all need to proclaim Jesus fearlessly. We need to be revived, renewed and empowered by the Holy Spirit to be

TIGERS FOR CHRIST

Preface

———◆———

It has been an enormous privilege for my wife and me to visit
South East Asian churches on a number of occasions during
the past ten years. We have a great admiration for what they
are achieving in the face of phenomenal difficulties: difficulties arising from language, culture, national diversities, lack
of resources, opposition and rank persecution. We have spent
quality time in all four dioceses which go to make up the
province of South East Asia, and have been privileged to
become close friends with their leadership. Twice I have led
the two-day retreat for the provincial synod prior to their
deliberations. I cannot claim to be intimate with their concerns, but I can claim to have a good visitor's overview of
what is happening in this very exciting part of the world
where the Christian gospel, not least in its Anglican form, is
growing apace.

I want to acknowledge my great dependence in the follow-
ing pages on a number of books published in South East Asia
but not readily accessible in the West. I think particularly of
Singapore: The Church in the Midst of Change, James Wong,
Church Growth Study Centre, Singapore, 1973; *Not Alone*,
Diocesan Women's Board, Singapore, 1995; *You Called Me*,
Clergy Testimonies, Singapore, 1998; *Rise Up: Go Forward*,
ed. Jonathan Wong, Logos, 1999; *Love Singapore*, Singapore
1999; *Visions Unfold*, Singapore, 1999; *Growing Churches –
Singapore Style*, Keith Hinton, Overseas Missionary Fellowship, 1985; and *150 Years of the Anglican Church in Borneo*,
ed. Peter Mulok Kedit, Lee Ming Press, 1998. I count it an
enormous privilege to have been associated with the Anglican
Church in this part of the world during its formative shift

into an independent Province of the Anglican Communion, and I am deeply appreciative of the welcome constantly given me by its leaders. This book draws heavily on the authorities quoted above, and on personal interviews. The mistakes in fact and perspective are my responsibility alone. I am deeply grateful for the help of Mr Rob Merchant, a colleague at Wycliffe Hall, who has read the manuscript. I offer this short book in the hope that it may stimulate the Church in the West to learn from its cousins in South East Asia, where the gospel is growing at such a remarkable pace.

Michael Green
Wycliffe Hall, Oxford University
Easter 2000

1

Learning from South East Asia

The Anglican Province of South East Asia has only been in existence since 1996 but it must be one of the fastest growing parts of the Anglican Communion. This is partly due to the fact that it is a small and relatively cohesive Province, embracing four contiguous dioceses and touching eight countries. It is certainly partly due to the fact that the church is vigorously facing the religious pluralism all around. It is equally certainly due to dynamic leadership. But on any showing the fact remains that the whole Province is growing fast, whereas figures in Britain and America indicate that the Anglican Church continues to be in serious decline. Could it be that Christians in the West have something to learn from their Asian counterparts?

Before the usual excuses spring to mind, namely that you cannot compare growth in the Two-Thirds World with the First World, or a developing society with a postmodern industrial one, let us be clear what we are doing. We are not comparing two totally dissimilar situations. Singapore is one of the most densely populated urban societies in the world. It is multicultural, with three major races and religions living cheek-by-jowl in its streets and its high rises. It has a deliberate civic policy of religious pluralism: indeed that is far more *de rigeur* than it is in Britain. It is on the cutting edge of information technology and is a highly developed industrial society with a massive port. Moreover, English is the main language, and Singapore follows the British parliamentary model, legal system, marriage law and customs, and educational system – and her young population is infatuated with Western pop music, rather than traditional Chinese music.

In other words, Singapore has much in common with Britain.

Much, but not all. For Singapore has been independent only since 1965, when her two-year honeymoon as part of the Federation of Malaysia ended abruptly: she was expelled, because her Chinese majority was rightly seen to be a threat to Malay supremacy. At that stage, her existence hung on as slender a thread as did Britain's in the Battle of Britain. For the island was a densely populated, squalid slum, with no obvious resources, no natural hinterland, little industry or internal markets, chronic unemployment and widespread corruption and vice.

There were other problems. The ethnic divisions in her society, closely allied to economic distinctions, led to a lot of misunderstandings and some riots. Of the population, 77 per cent were Chinese, many of whom had become wealthy and powerful. The 15 per cent of Malays were far less influential than in West Malaysia, and the 7 per cent of Indians were on the whole the least privileged members of the population. But that subdivision is itself too simplistic. The Chinese came from at least five dialect groups – Hakka, Hainanese, Cantonese, Teochew and Hokkien. The Indians were equally disparate, some coming from Sri Lanka, some from Pakistan and some from Nepal. Even the Malays were far from homogeneous, coming as they did from Javanese, Minang and Batak roots. There were at least four major languages in daily operation: English, Mandarin, Malay and Tamil. It was hard, indeed, to create an effective society or church from such disparate building-blocks.

But Singapore had two major advantages – a strong, visionary leadership, and an intelligent and hardworking people. It is the combination of these two that has made it the outstanding industrial community that it is. In a few decades Singapore has completely rebuilt one of the most densely populated slums in the world, relocated three-quarters of her population in modern, high-rise housing estates. She has almost full employment, enviable educational facilities, low inflation and a massive surplus in balance of payments.

Singapore is now one of the most important ports in the world and one of its most significant financial centres. Her technological skills help many nations, and her national airline and telecommunications reach worldwide. Far from being an undeveloped state, Singapore can compete with anywhere on the planet.

It is for this reason that Singapore invites comparison with Britain, and the Anglican Church there with the church in the UK. It is certainly no easier for the church to grow in Singapore than it is in Britain; indeed, its advance in recent years started from a position far behind that of Britain, where there is an Anglican church on every corner, thousands of clergy, more than 1 million weekly worshippers, and considerable (if depleted) financial resources. Moreover, Christianity has been the traditional faith of Britain for nearly two thousand years. On any showing, Singapore should not have been as effective in church growth as Britain, yet she far outpaces us. It is clearly important for those concerned with mission in Britain to pay attention to what is happening in Singapore.

As well as Singapore, I want to at least allude in this study to the Anglican Church in the other three dioceses of the Province, namely West Malaysia, Sabah and Kuching. Though all three dioceses are less urbanized than Singapore, they have close connections, and their churches run on rather similar lines. Since 1996 when the Anglican churches were formed into the Province of South East Asia, they have worked closely together, and all have been influenced greatly by the charismatic or renewal movement. This applies not only to their membership but in a large degree to their bishops, who have offered distinguished leadership. I recall that at the time of the 1988 Lambeth Conference, Bishop Moses Tay was invited to contribute to the pre-Lambeth collection of papers. In it he expressed views which can only be called evangelical and charismatic. And I recall expressions of profound dissent in the church press from the traditional Anglican churches in other parts of the region. This would not happen today. There is an openness to the Holy Spirit and a dependence on his powerful intervention in the churches of all four countries. However, in Anglican circles at least, the charismatic movement began in Singapore, and speedily embraced the bishop himself. It may be significant to trace some of the early streams which flowed into what is now a broad river of renewal.

The streams that made for renewal

Perhaps the first was the appointment of an indigenous bishop. It seems amazing that this was so long delayed, considering that there had been an Anglican presence in Singapore since 1826, when Sir Stamford Raffles appointed Robert Burns as the first chaplain of this British trading post in the Far East. The appointment was thoroughly overdue, but when it came, it opened up a new chapter in the life of the church in Singapore. Bishop Chiu Ban It was consecrated the first Malaysian-born (albeit English-educated) bishop of Singapore in 1966.

In his inaugural sermon, Bishop Chiu stressed four ideals which he hoped would characterize the Church, under the acronym PEWS. He looked for a growth in prayer, evangelism, witness and service. By the grace of God he was able to see all four begin to materialize during the years when he led the diocese from 1966–1982. It was he who launched the 'Know your Scriptures' campaign, a three-year programme designed to make lay people biblically literate, and to help them relate the teaching of the Bible to contemporary daily life. He was fortunate to secure the help of Bishop Stephen Neill, the distinguished missionary bishop, author and Bible scholar. He both taught workshops to give an overview of the Bible, and equipped Bible study leaders to make use of his materials through weekend courses. These groups developed in different churches, especially the cathedral, and in due course led into the Lay Training Course for which Singapore Anglicanism has subsequently become celebrated.

The appointment of an indigenous bishop and the new emphasis on the Bible were two of the important factors that lay behind the renewal in Singapore. A third was vigorous youth work. A report to the Synod in 1970 shared the concern that the number of youth fellowship members was so small as to be alarming. At this time members of the Anglican Church in Singapore were as slow to read the signs of the times as others were in Britain. Young people comprised 54 per cent of the population of Singapore, 21 per cent of them between the ages of 12 and 21. They were therefore a vitally important part of the population if the gospel was to advance. A youth secretary was appointed to co-ordinate and develop the work among young people in Singapore. He had to face a good deal of suspicion from older members who foresaw the young people bringing 'bongo drums and other devilish devices into the church, having free prayers and abolishing the Scripture readings'. Well, the drums and free prayer have certainly taken root, though Scripture retains a prominent place! The youth work in Singapore is outstanding, and it began with this clear vision and courageous implementation in the early 1970s.

A fourth factor in preparing the way for the contemporary advance was the way the Synod in Singapore enthusiastically embraced and backed the recommendation of the 1968 Lambeth Conference that 'Christians duly baptised in the name of the Holy Trinity and qualified to receive Holy Communion in their own churches, may be welcomed at the Lord's table in the Anglican Communion'. This made an enormous difference in breaking down denominational barriers in the island and helping Christians to recognize their joint membership of the same family of God.

But the overwhelming avenue for renewal came with the bishop himself. In the early 1970s the worldwide charismatic movement reached Singapore, producing a good deal of initial confusion and uncertainty. Some Anglicans enthusiastically embraced it; others were profoundly sceptical, not least among them the Chinese Christians, who had been burnt by some painful previous experiences years earlier, with the extreme claims and doubtful orthodoxy of a charismatic Chinese actress, Kong Mui Yee. I remember my first visit to Singapore, and St Andrew's Cathedral when I was myself beginning to experience the benefits of this new movement. I found a stone wall among the Chinese clergy in the cathedral, which was dominated by traditional Anglican services, indifferent congregations and culturally inappropriate English cathedral music, such as Merbecke plainsong, for the eucharist. Not surprisingly, the vibrant forms of worship, the freedom and the lay involvement of the early charismatics found scant favour. But the prayer in tongues, the prophetic utterances, the expectant prayers for healing and the sheer enthusiasm raised more serious questions. Could this be, as the *Straits Times* (2 November 1972) wondered, 'an unhealthy cult spreading among the young'? That is how it appeared to many in the early days, with all the mistakes that were made in the first flush of a new discovery of the power and presence of the Holy Spirit.

But soon this new enthusiasm was spreading fast, not only among the young people, but among increasing numbers of the older members of the churches. Lay Christians experienced for themselves the release of the Spirit in their lives, the new joy and boldness in witness, the new empowering to live an attractive Christian life and take risks for God. Many of them spoke in tongues, prayed for healings (and often saw them) and became effective in ministry to one another. The new songs embodied a living experience of God, and had easy catchy tunes. They did not have much theology behind them, or the spiritual depth of some of the greatest hymns of the past, but the new songs expressed the new vitality of today's renewed people of God. As a result, new 'charismatic' Anglican churches sprang into being and attracted a substantial following. At the same time, many in the more traditional Anglican churches had been touched by the Spirit in a fresh way, and this began gradually to emerge in the way the services were taken. Frequently those who were in some leadership position within their churches gained what was called at the time 'a taste of new wine', and through them the charismatic influence was introduced into the regular worship of the Church.

Such was the situation, vibrant but confused, when a remarkable thing happened to Bishop Chiu. He happened to be at a conference on salvation held at Bangkok in 1972. It was one of the most horizontal conferences it was possible to imagine. In the heyday of liberalism, salvation was being seen not in its broad biblical categories but in a narrowly liberationist mode: it meant financial and moral support for freedom fighters in countries which experienced oppressive regimes. Well, into this rather earthbound situation the living God broke through. Although hitherto wary of the renewal movement, Bishop Chiu had been handed a copy of the early charismatic Dennis Bennett's *Nine O'Clock in the Morning* and was impressed by the love and spiritual power of which it wrote. So he asked God to break into his own life with this power: 'Lord, if you can fill Dennis with your Holy Spirit and transform his ministry, can you please do the same for me?' And the Lord did, with an enormous impact, starting in the middle of that very night. He wrote:

> When I woke up I was conscious of a great difference within me. God was suddenly very close. My heart was filled with life, joy and peace instead of anger, despair and gloom. I burst out with praise and thanked God through Jesus Christ. When I ran out of English words I resorted to Chinese. Soon I was struggling again to find words and correct theological thoughts to express myself. The dam of the mind burst, and I found myself uttering new sounds and syllables which had no meaning to my mind but which I knew in my spirit were fluently giving expression to the praise and thanksgiving which was welling within me towards God.

That experience revolutionized the bishop's ministry. I had known him previously, and he was frankly weak. I had seen him roughly treated by clergy in his own synod, so much so that he went away overseas to his psychiatrist for treatment. But now he was a new man, aglow with the love and spiritual power of the Spirit of God. This was particularly noticeable in the ministry of healing and deliverance. I recall that he asked me back to his cathedral in 1973 after he had invited an overseas charismatic, Edgar Webb, to lead healing sessions there. These drew large crowds, and the bishop was drawn in to ministering personally among them – and found, to his amazement, that God had greatly gifted him in this area. When he invited me back to the cathedral to speak at the prayer service on a Friday night, I was astonished that anybody would come to pray then – judging by what I had seen in my previous visit. I was astounded to find the cathedral packed. I was asked to preach evangelistically, which I did. A good many people responded, and were led away to be counselled elsewhere: I never saw them again! Meanwhile Bishop Chiu preached a second sermon on healing, and invited people up to the rail for ministry. Many came, and I was amazed to see physical healings of an incontrovertible nature – I think of a man throwing away his crutches, and another whose hearing was restored. This was heady stuff, and the two of us retired to the bishop's house full of joy to praise God and eat a bedtime banana. It was then that he encouraged me to pray in tongues. I said that I could not do it – after all, I was British, an Oxford-trained academic, and a New Testament teacher. This was definitely not my scene! So we sat there rejoicing, and eating bananas, while he praised God in tongues and I praised him as best I could! He then prayed for me to receive the gift. Nothing happened, and we went to bed. In the middle of the night I awoke with the beginning of a gift of tongues, which has developed since, and has proved invaluable in my ministry.

Of course I only saw the tip of an iceberg during that visit, though I am constantly reminded of it, wearing, as I do, a watch bought for me on that occasion by the bishop. The reality was very far-reaching. The diocese was beginning to blaze with the fire of the Holy Spirit. New churches emerged, and there was one of those spontaneous advances of the gospel that nobody can organize but nobody can fail to note when it happens. The centre of all this activity was the cathedral itself, and it became a major resource for renewal in the whole island and beyond. Charismatic praise and prayer services became weekly events, along with seminars on the work of the Holy Spirit. These seminars went on for seven years and had an enormous influence among people of varying denominations in Singapore. Canon James Wong, one of the key figures in the renewal, commented on the effect of all this on the once strait-laced Anglican Church in Singapore.

> These healing services marked a turning point for the Anglican Church in Singapore and introduced a new dimension of power and life in the Spirit to the Church. Instead of being an inward-looking institution, the Anglican Church began to reach out to the lost, the sick and the needy, and offer life and reality to them by exalting Jesus Christ and introducing the Saviour to them. The gospel became alive to the Church. Signs and wonders accompanied the preaching of the gospel. This kind of power-evangelism became the Church's priority and mission as a result of the Renewal.

Needless to say the renewal movement was not welcomed by all sections of the Church, nor by the Anglicans in nearby dioceses such as Kuching and West Malaysia. The un-Anglican enthusiasm, the doctrinal weaknesses, the raised hands, new choruses, loud music and exaggerated claims, along with some divisive tendencies and traces of spiritual pride, naturally caused suspicion. And so they should. The charismatic movement can be chaotic unless it is based on a strong biblical theology and kept within a firm church framework.

So Bishop Chiu took pains to present to his synod in 1977 a careful analysis of the renewal movement. He welcomed the work of the Spirit in the Anglican Church of Singapore, but he also laid down wise criteria for discerning truth from error. Of any claim for something to be the work of the Holy Spirit he encouraged people to ask seven questions:

1. Is it consistent with Holy Scripture?
2. Is it motivated by 'agape' love?
3. Is it for the common good?
4. Is it accompanied by the fruit of the Spirit?
5. Does it guide into truth?
6. Does it glorify Jesus?
7. Does the spirit behind it, when tested, affirm that Jesus is the incarnate Son of God?

Wise advice. And equally wise was his support for the Lambeth Conference resolutions on 'The Holy Spirit and Renewal' and on 'Healing', which welcomed the current resurgence of the work of the Spirit and declared that healing the sick in the name of Jesus was as much a part of the gospel as preaching the good news of Jesus. In this time of acute change, Bishop Chiu had the wisdom to give equal emphasis both to the inherited sacramental worship of the Church and to the new praise services. And he refused to go down the triumphalist path of some charismatics who suggested that the power of the Spirit exempted us from disease or guaranteed success in life. Equally, he safeguarded against extravagant charismatic claims by stressing the importance of the careful and scholarly study of Holy Scripture, and of testing everything by it. That is, of course, the historic attitude of Anglicanism, following as it does the thrust of the Thirty Nine Articles: 'Holy Scripture containeth all things necessary to salvation: so that whatsoever is not read therein, nor may be proved thereby, is not to be required of any man, that it should be believed as an article of the faith' (Article 6).

The diocese made enormous advances during this period of major renewal presided over by Bishop Chiu. Discerning friends could only marvel. For Bishop Chiu was not a natural leader. Before his deep infilling with the Holy Spirit he was weak, but thereafter he proved to be a marvellous example of

God's power made perfect in weakness. And he himself tells us the secret of his effectiveness. 'The Lord made it very clear to me that he wanted his Church back. The Diocese of Singapore was not mine, with him helping, but his with me helping! When I humbly submitted to him he began to do great things in the Diocese and Church of Singapore.' I can add my own 'Amen' to that testimony. I witnessed both his humility and his power in serving the Lord, and in a variety of visits I saw some of the remarkable fruit that emerged. The humility, the new experience of the Holy Spirit and the consequent effectiveness of Bishop Chiu have been a powerful pointer to me about the nature of true Christian leadership. He was small enough for God to fill and use, unlike many bishops who, sadly, become prelatical in their attitudes, formal in their churchmanship and seem to imagine that they own their dioceses. The Chiu years were years of extraordinary revitalizing for the Anglican Church in Singapore. By the time he retired to England in 1982 the stage was set for a major advance along the path he had pioneered. All that was needed was a strong, Spirit-filled leader. And God led the diocese to choose one, in the person of Moses Tay.

The renewal that burst its banks

Chiu Ban It had a remarkable vision while he was in office. He saw a well overgrown with weeds and holding little water. When he asked the Lord what he should do about it, the reply was that the drought is a good time to clear out the well, for when the rains come the well will not be able to contain all the water. Yet the bishop himself was not to be the one to build the new well. That would be the task of someone else.

And so it proved. The Rev. Dr Moses Tay, a hospital superintendent and non-stipendiary minister who was ordained only four years earlier, was elected bishop – in painful circumstances, because his wife died before his consecration. He soon showed what he was made of. He built on the foundation Ban It had left him, but threw all his clear-headedness, mental toughness and organizational ability into the work. He was very keen to see the four dioceses combined into the new Province of South East Asia, and this was achieved, after various tribulations, in 1996, when he was appointed the first archbishop. It was long before this, how-ever, that his main contributions to the tremendous growth of the Church became evident. I think they fall into four cat-egories, leadership, mission, community involvement and conviction, all crucial for spiritual advance. They stand out all the more clearly because they are often missing in the West.

Leadership

The first was his emphasis on leadership. Singapore became a byword for training ordained and lay leaders for the Church. As regards the clergy, Moses Tay was more concerned that his should be converted, full of the Holy Spirit, with a lively confidence in the Scriptures and a deep love for people, than that they should have gone through the inherited ordi-nation preparation. This led to some tension between him and Singapore's Trinity Theological College. He was prepared to ordain applicants for the ministry if they had been to Bible college rather than seminary, and this led to an effective 'hands-on' type of leadership rather than one deeply versed in theology. This produced short-term strengths but may lead to long-term weaknesses.

It was in his training for leadership among lay people that the bishop's true vision and greatness was seen. He built on and co-ordinated existing training to develop a threefold and very comprehensive plan.

The first part started with enquirers into the Christian faith and went right through conversion and initial nurture, to confirmation preparation and confirmation. He built into this a systematic plan for reading the New Testament. Every church member was encouraged to go through this programme, and the vast majority did. By 1989 10,884 had completed this first part of a visionary scheme to begin to equip large numbers of well-instructed lay leaders for the Church.

The second part focused on equipping lay Christians for different aspects of ministry. It was founded on the apostolic premise that all Christians are called to minister to Christ, not just some. And the function of the ordained ministry was seen by Moses Tay, as by St Paul, to be primarily that of enabling the church members to discover and carry out the particular ministry within the body of Christ for which the Holy Spirit had equipped them. This Diocesan Lay Training Programme, first introduced in conjunction with the Diocesan Mission in 1984, was conducted at a parish level but co-ordinated by the diocese. Carefully selected teachers created the three-part programme which leads in due course to a Diploma in Ministry. Part One comprises a ten-week course of practical, 'How to' modules; a Certificate of Lay Ministry is awarded to those who complete it. Part Two comprises twelve units, covering the whole Bible; those who complete this demanding programme are awarded the Certificate of Biblical Studies. Part Three is partly residential, and majors on more advanced areas of Christian discipleship, leadership and various aspects of church management, church planting and church growth. Those who complete this course are awarded the Certificate of Church Ministry.

There is nothing static about this Diploma. For example, Diocesan Children's Ministry units were added to the pro-gramme, and this has led to thousands of well-trained youth and children's workers. Bishop Tay took a great deal of per-sonal interest in this, and when in due course he married again, his wife Cynthia became closely associated with the programme. Her deep spirituality, personal warmth and biblical understanding contributed enormously to its growth and effectiveness.

Where in the Anglican world is there anything remotely comparable to this superb training programme? And where in the world is there a general level among church members of comparable biblical insight, practical skills and evangelistic and pastoral concern? They are far ahead of the rest of us, and we in the West need to learn from them that we will never have effective churches if we do not entertain comprehensive training programmes to equip our people.

Mission and evangelism

There was a particular need for this in Singapore. And the passion of the diocese at large and its bishop in particular was for evangelism and mission. The home cells which had begun under his predecessor became very numerous under Bishop Moses. They supplemented, and did not supplant, the regular Sunday worship of the churches. Small groups of a dozen or so, meeting weekly in homes, were led by lay men or women, normally those who had gone through the entire Diocesan Lay Training Programme. These cells proved invaluable in many ways. They cut down on backsliding, since all church members were encouraged to belong to one. They developed leadership skills. They were a natural and easy vehicle for evangelism, for many who would never go near a church were happy enough to go along to a home group when invited by a good friend. They alerted members to the social needs in their immediate vicinity, which they tried to meet. They were ideal for building up young Christians and in due course for supporting missionary ventures into other countries. Of course, if you are going to major on small 'cell' groups like this, you have got to have competent leaders. And that is what the Diocesan Lay Training course sought to produce, and where to a marvellous degree it succeeded. We shall have much more to say about cell groups in a subsequent chapter. Sufficient here to note that this became one of the major ways in which the gospel spread throughout the island. They are so prolific that by 2002 the churches in Singapore expect to have a cell in every street and every high-rise housing block.

This passion for evangelization which has so characterized Archbishop Moses' episcopate was not confined to the island of Singapore. It is far more widespread than that. He realized that the little Province of South East Asia was set in a position rather like the church at Philadelphia in the book of Revelation. The Christ who is 'the holy one, the true one, who has the key of David, who opens and no one will shut, who shuts and no one opens says, "I know your works. Look, I have set before you an open door, which no one is able to shut. I know that you have but little power, and yet you have kept my word and have not denied my name"' (Revelation 3.8). In the early days they had very limited power and resources in the Anglican Church in Singapore. But they gave it everything they had. The archbishop appointed some of his senior clergy as deans of the adjoining countries (when there were as yet no Anglicans there!). That was an astonishingly bold and visionary thing to do. Thus James Wong became Dean of Indonesia, Norman Beale of Nepal, Gerald Khoo of Thailand, and John Benson of Laos and Cambodia. They were all commissioned to start an Anglican work from scratch. Have you heard of such a thing in the West? I know that I have not. I salute this truly apostolic spirit. Most of these men are having to learn the languages in question and are entering the countries on short-term visitors' permits because nothing more permanent is allowed them. Six months later they go again, on another visitor's pass. In due course Christians from these countries are brought to Singapore (also on visitors' visas!) for training and perhaps, in due course, ordination. And all this has happened in the past few years as a direct result of the evangelistic fire that burns in the heart of the archbishop.

Nor is this the whole story. The gospel has been well established in West Malaysia, Kuching and Sabah for a long time, and these dioceses have become vital partners in the work of the new Province. Encouraging visits for church renewal and training, coming primarily from Singapore, have contributed greatly to the fire that is burning so brightly in all three countries, and throughout the region. Mission is their lifeblood, and spiritual gifts their equipment.

Community involvement

One of the tragedies in the West, particularly since the great Edinburgh Missions Conference in 1910, is the most unfortunate division between those who see the gospel primarily in terms of proclamation and those who see it primarily in terms of practical service. The former have tended to be more theologically conservative, the latter more liberal. And in this way the divide has grown and there has been considerable acrimony on both sides. This is, of course, a terrible travesty of New Testament Christianity, where Jesus and his apostles *both* preached the kingdom of God *and* healed the sick and met the needs of the hungry. The division between the two emphases has harmed both, and rendered both inadequate representatives of what Jesus called his church to be.

Singapore has not fallen into that mistake. This vibrant, charismatic Christianity of Singapore is, like its earlier and more traditional manifestation, profoundly concerned with the community and dedicated to trying to meet its many needs. Nobody could say that it is 'happy and clappy', untouched by the pain of society round about. As early as 1842 the missionary Maria Dyer founded St Margaret's School for young girls who were in virtual slavery, and in 1862 St Andrew's Mission School for boys was founded by the Revd E. S. Venn. Education has been an important thrust of the Anglican presence ever since.

Although they are now government-aided, the Anglican schools still teach religious knowledge and hold regular chapel services, as well as permitting the students to hold their own informal gatherings for Bible reading, fellowship and prayer. One of the most significant aspects of this schools work is the counselling programme that the Anglican Church has put in place. It is enormously appreciated, especially among those who have learning difficulties, or come from a disturbed background. But the Church does not leave matters there. They have set up kindergartens and childcare centres as well.

Medical work has been another important thrust of the Church in Singapore. Here again the origins go far back. In 1914 Charlotte Ferguson-Davie, wife of the bishop, started two small clinics to reach the desperate needs of the impoverished women and children in the streets. By 1923 the St Andrew's Mission hospital was functioning, and other medical developments followed, with the Mission Hospital at Tanjong Pagar and the orthopaedic Hospital for Children in Siglap. Wherever the gospel has gone in the world it has been accompanied by true Christian concern for people's bodies, with medicine, and for their minds, with education. And so this medical work continues to grow. For example the Singapore Anglican Welfare Council runs a couple of centres for the mentally and emotionally disturbed. Crisis centres for battered women have sprung up. The cathedral runs a home for the aged, and the diocese has initiated the St Andrew's Lifestreams, which is a counselling centre to equip both church and community groups in counselling skills which can be used in Christian and in secular contexts.

Recently there has been a concentrated effort to 'Love Singapore'. This is a trans-denominational plan to express God's love throughout Singapore not primarily in words but in deeds. They have a motto: 'Small things done with great love will change the world.' It is a highly practical series of suggestions for showing the love of God in the neighbourhood where they live, and it is immensely attractive. Much more will be said about this in a subsequent chapter, and it is a very important area, not only because it is intrinsic to the gospel but also because many of the strategies they employ can readily be adapted to Britain.

But the main thing to notice at this point is that all the social and community work done by the Church in Singapore is an outworking of Christians' deep commitment to Christ, and they are not in the least afraid of mentioning his name as

the source of their inspiration and service. This stands in
sharp contrast to the situation which often prevails in the
West. For example, the Church of England has colleges of
education, but they do not seem to breed Christian teachers
any better than the secular colleges. With the shining excep-
tion of the Roman Catholic colleges, ours in the West are not
notable for turning out committed Christians. It is the same
in our medical and social work. It is almost as though we are
embarrassed to mention our Saviour. I shall never forget
when some Argentine Anglicans came to Vancouver, in the
Diocese of New Westminster, where I was working at the
time. They spread their enthusiastic expression of the faith
around wherever they went, and were duly impressed at
some of the social work being done by the Anglican Church
there. But they asked, 'And when do you tell them about
Jesus?' There was no answer to that question!

   We need to learn from our Asian friends that it is not
enough to give the cup of cold water: we need to do so in the
name of Jesus. That is what happens quite unashamedly in
Singapore. 'Serving the community is a major objective,'
wrote Archbishop Tay. 'It is part and parcel of the church's
ministry of meeting needs. We do this as an expression of
God's love. By participating in community service the
Church becomes relevant to the community.' It does indeed,
and Singapore shows its impact.

Conviction

Anybody who knows Moses Tay knows that he is a man of
strong conviction. If you do not like what he stands for, you
call him awkward, controversial and so on. If you do like it,
you see him as the champion of orthodoxy. I can claim to
know him rather well, and I am sure that his strength of
conviction comes from a genuine commitment to the teaching of the Scriptures. That is where all Christian leadership
should originate. Significantly, in the Anglican tradition, a
person is given a Bible at ordination, not a chalice and patten

as used to be the case before the Reformation. The priest has to swear allegiance to the teachings of the Bible as the supreme norm in Anglicanism. To be sure there are others as well, notably tradition, reason and the teachings of great Christians down the ages. But Scripture remains determinative. 'Do you accept the holy Scriptures as revealing all things necessary for eternal salvation through faith in Christ?' asks the bishop, and nobody is ordained unless they can say 'I do so accept them.' He is further asked, 'Will you be diligent in prayer, in reading holy Scripture, and in all studies that will deepen your faith and fit you to uphold the truth of the Gospel against error?' The candidate replies, 'By the help of God, I will.'

Precisely the same things are asked of those chosen to be bishops. Moreover in Britain, whenever a clergyman moves to another parish, the bishop reminds both the priest and the congregation that the faith is 'uniquely set forth in the Scriptures' and that the minister 'has a responsibility to maintain this witness'. The clergyman has to 'profess firm and sincere belief in the faith set forth in the Scriptures and in the catholic creeds, and allegiance to the doctrine of the Church of England'. Though sister churches of the Anglican Communion have slightly different forms of words in their ordination services, the cardinal importance of the scriptural basis for Christianity is maintained in them all. The sad thing is that many clergy make this profession but do not believe it and do not act on it. Moses Tay makes that profession and wholeheartedly believes it. And that is where his famed conservatism comes from. He is not conservative in practice – he is extremely imaginative and inventive, taking risks that would not be countenanced in many Provinces and generally making a glorious success of them. But he is conservative about Scripture. He is faithful to his ordination vows. He knows that these Scriptures were considered decisive by Jesus and by faithful Christians down the ages. He knows they have power to convert and nourish, to warn, encourage and build up. That is why he takes his stand upon them. And that is why he seems conservative, difficult and controversial to those who do not believe in the authority of Scripture. In lifestyle, he is modest. In language, courteous. In attitude, non-aggressive. In self-assessment, humble. But when other bishops are flagrantly opposing the manifest teaching of the Bible, he is as fearless as a lion.

In the 1988 Lambeth Conference he stood out against the ordination of women. This was hotly debated and eventually passed, but the conference allowed different Provinces to make their own decisions on the matter. This the Province of South East Asia did, and to this day it has no women presbyters. We may or may not approve of their stance, but the important thing to notice is that it was made not on the grounds of male chauvinism but of biblical principle. There is not a lot in the Bible to support the notion of women in leadership. There is some – women like Deborah in the Old Testament and Phoebe, Euodia, Syntyche and Priscilla in the New. But it is scanty enough. And throughout the Bible there is teaching on the headship that the husband is called upon to exercise over his wife. This was the biblical evidence that proved decisive for Moses and his fellow bishops in the Province. 'The issue is headship,' he declared. 'Whom has God ordained to head his churches? God created male and female, but he created Adam first. We believe the plain teachings of Scripture. The ordained clergy should be male.'

Now it may readily be allowed that the matter is a lot more complicated than that. The headship argument is profoundly changed by the way Jesus, the Lord and Master of his disciples, knelt to wash their feet. He went literally head-over-heels to serve them. And then he told them to adopt the same attitude to one another, thus modifying any authoritarian understanding of headship. It is a complicated issue on which Scripture is not as clear as we would wish, and Christians will weigh the evidence differently. But what nobody can deny is that Archbishop Moses and his colleagues were not influenced by tradition, culture, feminism or male chauvinism. They went to the Scriptures for their norms. They may have been wrong in their exegesis and hermeneutics. They were certainly right in their attitude of going back to the heart of the Christian faith, in the Scriptures.

The Lambeth Conference of 1998 will always be remembered for the intense battles over the ordaining of practising homosexuals and the conducting of same-sex unions. The climate of the day, particularly among the North American revisionist bishops, was actively libertarian, but had no basis whatsoever in Scripture. It was to the Scripture that Moses and his colleagues turned. They were berated, accused of intransigence, ignorance and being only a generation from witchcraft and savagery, but they stood fast. And they won the day – handsomely. To be sure, many of the American bishops behaved very disloyally, and returned home to denounce the Lambeth declaration and to go on ordaining practising homosexuals and in some cases dispossessing orthodox clergy of their churches because they took a biblical stance. This has produced the most serious problem ever for the continued existence of the Anglican Communion as we know it. It could well split apart over the issue, or perhaps the American Episcopal Church might even be ejected from the Anglican Communion.

A meeting of the Anglican Consultative Council was held in 1999. And the archbishop of the Province of South East Asia and his fellow bishops refused to attend, because it was taking place in Scotland, hosted by its Primus, Bishop Holloway, who was one of the most passionate and, I am sorry to say, discourteous advocates of homosexual unions. A lot of wrath descended on Moses Tay's head. To stay away was, after all, hardly the way to conduct a civilized debate! But the day of civilized debate had been developed at great length during the recent Lambeth Conference, and a decision arrived at by a massive majority. Yet here was Bishop Holloway, a provincial head, openly flaunting the homosexual banner, in defiance of that Lambeth resolution on sexuality. Moreover, his denunciation of opponents and statements in the press rendered him widely unacceptable to the clergy in his own diocese, and he has since resigned. Why, then, should it be thought inappropriate for an orthodox archbishop to decide he had had enough and would be no part or parcel of this conference? I cannot fault him for it. Can you? That is leadership; costly, principled, unpopular leadership. The Anglican Church rightly values comprehensiveness and collegiality, but is also in grave need of courageous leadership. Some have criticized him on the grounds that Moses Tay should have waited until the Conference of Anglican Primates in March 2000, but by that time he would have passed on the archiepiscopal mantle.

If he was to make a stand for orthodoxy, this was the time to make it. He did. Indeed, he went further. At the end of January 2000 he, along with Archbishop Kolini of Rwanda and various other bishops, took the unprecedented step of consecrating two senior and orthodox American clergymen to be missionary bishops in the USA but accountable to the Provinces of Rwanda and South East Asia. This has caused a tremendous furore, the implications of which are still far from clear at the time of writing. He did it at the request of orthodox, believing Anglican clergy in America, who were being harassed and in some cases ejected from their parishes by liberal or 'revisionist' bishops, determined to press ahead with homosexual ordinations and to brook no opposition from traditional clergy. The revisionists were only too happy to keep the debate going, while proceeding with their agenda, which was disloyal to Scripture, their own canons and the resolutions of the Lambeth Conference. Moses Tay responded to the cry for help from the marginalized orthodox minority in the Episcopal Church of the USA. He ceased talking, which had proved useless, and acted. He may be excoriated or applauded for so doing. One thing is certain. He is a standing example of the true adage 'Leaders must lead'.

Referring to the significance of Archbishop Moses Tay in the Anglican Communion, the assistant bishop of Singapore, John Tan, said, 'We may be a small province but we need to be a champion of biblical orthodoxy. This voice for orthodoxy serves as a clarion call for others to wake up and realize what is wrong with the Church today. It is a dam against biblical liberalism and attacks on the Bible.'

It seems to me that as we in the West review the growth in Singapore, we have a reasonable record of social involvement, though not perhaps with the imagination and Christ-centredness that you find in the Province of South East Asia. But we do not take congregational training with anything like their seriousness. Our bishops and clergy are not, on the whole, famed, as theirs are, for a strong biblical orthodoxy. Our leaders do not often give a strong and fearless lead in matters of public debate. Ours is a culture of committees, not of strong leadership. As for that passion for missions and evangelism which characterizes the Eastern church, its fire splutters and grows dim in most of the West, with certain glorious exceptions. We are not prepared to preach unwelcome truths. We are not prepared to confront the idols of the day and the tenets of political correctness. In a word, we are not prepared to stand up for unvarnished biblical Christianity with all the energy we can muster. We are unwilling to face the sacrifice and contumely that would involve. In the areas of leadership, evangelism and orthodoxy we desperately need to learn lessons from South East Asia, and incorporate them appropriately into our own church culture.

2

Learning about Love

———◆———

Christians are meant to know about love. After all, it lies at the heart of what our faith is about. But we do not find it very easy. The Greeks had their problems about it, too. In fact, they had three different words for it. *Storge* was their word for love within the family, *philia* for love between friends, and *eros* for erotic love. But the first Christians instinctively understood that the love of God was different again. They dug up a word that had hardly ever been used in secular Greek, *agape*. A new word for a new concept – God's love which comes to us lavishly, free, with no strings attached. Love of that quality is enriching. It makes you stand tall. And Christians are meant not just to receive it and rejoice in it, but to show it to other people. Ah, there's the rub! And nowhere do we find it harder than in the little matter of evangelism – which is supposed to mean spreading the good news of God's love to all and sundry. Unfortunately what often comes across is not this warm, enriching, love but some rather different message. Like 'Come to church' or 'Adopt these moral standards' or 'Respond to this altar call'. No wonder people are slow to respond to that sort of thing. Can you blame them?

In Singapore the major churches are co-operating in taking a very different approach. They are seeking so to demonstrate the love of God in action that people are amazed and want to know its source. In other words, practical love plants a question mark in the heart of the recipient, and when you have a question mark there you are more than half way to helping them discover Jesus Christ, the supreme lover.

Of course, Christian love in action is as old as the gospel

itself. As we saw in the last chapter, the Church set out to educate minds and heal bodies in Singapore from its early days as a trading post. But with the project 'Love Singapore' it has become much more imaginative and clearly focused. In this chapter I propose to look quite carefully at what they are doing, and see what it has to teach us in our attempts to show the kindness of God to the people around us.

The vision that drives them

Let us first get a hold of their vision. It is breathtaking. Not a matter of increasing the numbers in their churches but of claiming the whole of Singapore for Christ. Several quite well grounded theological perceptions underlie this surprising goal. In the first place, they are clear on the sovereignty of God. He really is Lord of the whole earth. And currently we live in the kingdom of Christ, awaiting 'the end, when he hands over the kingdom to God the Father, after he has destroyed every ruler and every authority and power. For he must reign until he has put all his enemies under his feet' (1 Corinthians 15.24f.). We live in what Oscar Cullmann has called the Regnum Christi, which will one day usher in the Regnum Dei, the Reign of God. Very well, it follows from this premise that Singapore is Christ's country, his territory. Much of it does not acknowledge his sway. Much of it is in rebel hands. But Christ is the rightful ruler.

The second theological conviction which mobilizes the Singaporean church is this. God has appointed us to live in particular places. Jeremiah and Ezekiel understood this of Babylon. The Israelites were to seek the good of the place into which they had been taken captive. Paul underlines it in his Athenian address where he reminds them that God has determined 'the times of their existence and the boundaries of the places where they would live'(Acts 17.26). This means that we are not living in our particular location by accident but, whether we know it or not, it is the place God in his inscrutable wisdom has assigned to us.

The third very clear principle which stands out in the Great Commission and elsewhere is that the followers of Jesus are his ambassadors and are charged to make disciples worldwide. This could be so vague that we never do anything about it. But St Paul once again furnishes a helpful clue, in 2 Corinthians 10.13–16. 'We, however, will not boast beyond proper limits, but will keep within the field [i.e. territory or sphere of influence] God has assigned to us, to reach out even as far as you . . . We do not boast beyond our limits, that is, in the labours of others . . . of work already done in someone else's sphere of action. "Let the one who boasts boast in the Lord."' Paul is clear that a territory has been assigned him to work, and that is his first priority. It is the same with us. We have a responsibility to shine for God among the people in the area where we live. That is our first call.

So these committed Singaporean Christians believe that in a sense they already share in the reign of Christ over their particular area, and that Christ has given them all the resources they need to reach and win the people there. *They make a territorial commitment to their community.* This is of the utmost importance, and constitutes a complete paradigm shift. The walls between church and community come down, and the community, not church activities, becomes their focus. Their aim is no longer simply to fill their church but to win their community for its rightful King. These are the convictions, coupled with a deep compassion for lost people, which energize 'Love Singapore'. And these convictions lead into very decisive action, which they maintain is eminently achievable.

They set out to win the city-state for Christ, not just to grow a congregation. This means partnership, not competition between congregations and denominations. It means Kingdom building, not empire building. It means that the priority is not to attract transfer growth but to go all-out for conversion growth.

Moreover, their philosophy is to love and serve the community with no strings attached. This involves not only the principles, long accepted in the West, that evangelism is a process and not a crisis, and also that we must earn the right to speak. It goes further, because it manifests something of the loving heart of God. These Singaporean Anglicans are after nothing less than the transformation of their community, and that takes time. Premature preaching will merely alienate most people. Acts of love will progressively drive back the blindness and hardness of heart which keeps people from Christ. They have an acronym for it, SHOW, which stands for 'Softening Hearts and Opening Windows'.

Naturally, a project of this magnitude must involve the whole congregation. If the pastor is a superstar, then the congregation is likely to be an audience and not an army. They are in the business of mobilizing and equipping an army. The aim of this army is to see a changed community where the presence of Christ is experienced in the social, economic, political and spiritual arenas. And this can only happen when the whole church in an area makes a focused attempt to disciple, train and equip every member for maturity, and to be a flavour of Christ in the area.

What a goal! It is truly revolutionary. It will mean that the congregation comes to see that the impact on the community, not the hour on Sunday, is the purpose of the Church. They will begin to realize that ministry is not performing an act but influencing lives. It is about investing in people, not simply performing religious activity. And this impact on the community can only effectively be achieved through the loving effect of small groups of single-minded, loving Christians, acting naturally and in a variety of ways.

It will mean that the small groups or 'cells' in the church must own and flow with the vision of the whole church. In other words they must accept some direction, and not merely do their own thing. These small groups are not freewheeling entities, but sections in a platoon of God's army, out to establish a beachhead in different parts of the vicinity. This they do by 'owning' a small sector of the city or a high-rise block and concentrating on it, praying for the residents, seeking to get to know them and do them kindness, not just once but consistently 'until the harvest arrives'. It will mean that the goal of the church leadership changes. Instead of the traditional shepherd role the clergy will begin to adopt a prophetic or apostolic role. They will concentrate not so much on keeping their flock happy as on harnessing the energies of the congregation for loving, serving and reaching the people in their 'territory'.

The whole shape of the leadership is bound to change, given a goal of this magnitude. In the inherited mode of doing church, we have depended very much on the ordained priest to do almost everything. They see a big change here, as the emerging church moves from the 'positional to the relational to the functional'. That is to say that they no longer rely on the 'separate' status of the ordained minister. His task is to be a coach to the team, and this will inevitably involve a collegiate, relational role. Out of that will come clear evidence of the different gifts God has given to particular members of the church, and these gifts must be allowed to surface. Accordingly, there will be a strategic restructuring of leadership so that the best person for the job leads every operation. 'Authority that comes from optimum effectiveness based on gifting and anointing is slowly replacing the old paradigm of authority and seniority being measured by the hierarchy in the organization.' Obviously sensible, but what a revolution in the way a church operates! Just ask yourself – does your church function that way?

This shift of vision to a 'community-taking church' has other implications, many of them radical. It will mean that the church reaches out in an integrated way, men, women and children together, each contributing the gifts and talents that God has entrusted to them. It will mean that relationships become eloquent, as Christian families join in outreach together. It will mean that much of the church budget will need to be reassigned – so that, as they graphically put it, 'there is a growing expenditure on the lost rather than the saved'. That will prove a very challenging change, but it is essential if the church is going to be financially capable of showering love upon people in their area. Imagine giving away half the income of your church on lavishing generosity upon non-members!

It will mean that prayer becomes a top priority, for without it the powers of darkness will never be driven back. This is God's work, but he acts in response to the prayers of his people. In the West we do not know very much about this battling in prayer.

Naturally, the more the church represents a social, racial and economic mix the more effectively it will represent the Kingdom of God and the more attractive it will be to the huge variety of people that live in any one area. That is the sort of church the Singaporean Anglicans deliberately seek to be.

A feature that I found fascinating was the way in which these dynamic churches in Singapore see the need turning into the call. They have a new way of looking at our Christian vocation. Rather than allow their 'calling' to determine the direction and limits of their ministry, they see the community needs as constituting their calling. They are therefore very proactive, willing to take on the challenge of the hour. 'Yet charisma is never placed above character; talent cannot replace tenacity; and giftedness never supersedes godliness.'

The sobering challenge is this. Can we, dare we make the strategic paradigm shift and change the way we 'do church'? Robert Warren has pointed the way, but who is actually doing it? Are we willing to bring renewal to our wineskins so that we can contain and pass on to thirsty people the new wine God is providing in our day and generation? It will require real faith. And without faith it is impossible to please God or to achieve anything worthwhile for him.

Granted these convictions and this willingness for radical change, how do they actually go about it?

The patterns they adopt

They are very practical and intentional about it all. 'Vision can only happen when we have vehicles to move us towards the end-goal in mind.' They suggest five steps to 'community taking'. The first is *Open Highways*. Once the cell in the church takes territorial responsibility for a block, they get praying. They pray on site as much as possible, and expect to see cold disinterest and spiritual blindness gradually driven back.

Open Hands is the second step, as they come in the role of the servant to their chosen community and see how they can show appropriate acts of kindness to them. *Open Homes* is the third step. Cell members try to make a profile of the community by knocking on doors and asking what the residents feel are the major needs in the community. This information is then carefully compiled and then becomes fuel for prayer and spurs for action. Moreover it brings church people into face-to-face contact with the residents. *Open Hearts* is, hopefully, the next step. People will be softened by these acts of love, and their hearts will become increasingly open first to the messengers and then to the message that they bring. Step five is *Open Heavens*. By now when a felt need emerges and the Christians are trusted, there will be opportunities to pray with the residents. And they record many examples of healing, deliverance from evil spiritual forces, changed attitudes, conversions and new cells being planted.

Such is the plan, in outline. Let us look at it more closely.

1. Prayer

This is clearly top priority with them, but how do they go about it? They believe that intercessory prayer is not meant to be our last resort, but our first response to any situation. It is the essential weapon of every believer. It is the Christian activity that identifies us most closely with our Lord. It is not an art or a technique, but a cry from the heart to the Lord for others. It is vital for clergy to model intercessory prayer as the mainspring of their life and ministry. Only then does it take root in the members of their congregations. And they have discovered the power of prayer when it springs from united vision and action. One of the major thrusts of 'Love Singapore' is the unity among churches, Anglican and others, that it fosters as together they seek to minimize their differences and maximize obedience to their Lord's commission. They encourage private prayer, *closet prayer* as they sometimes call it. They encourage *cluster prayer* as a small group gets together to intercede. This can include prayerwalking and prayer triplets, of which more anon. They encourage *congregational prayer* – times when the congregation meets for intercession. And they make good use of *concerts of prayer*, bringing together churches from a variety of backgrounds to praise the Lord and pray for the city and the country. Let us glance at some of these different forms of intercession in greater detail.

Prayerwalking is simply intentional intercessory prayer, conducted on site, usually by several people, who are open to any insight they may receive from God. It means praying in the selected area for that community, praying in the very places where you look for answers. As for praying with insight, this can be of at least three kinds: pray for who and what you observe as you walk around; pray for what you discover about the community through library research, surveys or interviews; and pray for what the Holy Spirit may reveal to you.

Cell members normally form a small team, walk around the streets of their area observing and praying, and finish with a discussion of what they have perceived, and where further prayer might be concentrated. They find it helpful to begin corporately with prayers acknowledging the Lord's sovereignty, leading naturally into repentance. Then they claim the power of the ascended Christ over all the principalities and powers that oppose him, and intercede for what they long to happen in the area. They are careful to observe what is going on, and to give space for silence in order to allow God to speak. They seek to act in a priestly role, sensing the sins and struggles of the community and offering them to God in prayer. They take trouble to pray for those in authority locally, and to cry to God for the softening of hearts and his blessing on the community. Naturally they pray with eyes open and do not have a great phalanx of people going round together! The prayerwalking needs to be natural, unobtrusive and sensitive. Increasingly this is becoming a powerful weapon not just in the Far East but in England. In a recent citywide mission in which six teams were involved, by far the greatest response was encountered in the Area where there was persistent prayerwalking. Alas, it was not my Area! I hope I learned from the experience.

Congregational Prayer. Many churches in the West are nourished by a weekly prayer meeting. But there are other ways of making congregational prayer come alive. One is to include a 15-minute prayer slot into the Sunday service. Cut down the non-essentials to make room for this powerful essential. Many churches in Singapore make this a regular part of their Sunday worship, encouraging maximum participation, either in small groups or in plenary. Some churches even have everyone praying at once – an amazing and powerful experience, common in Korea. After all, God can sort it out. It removes embarrassment and it gives everyone a chance! It is good to have a clear theme for the occasion, and to vary that theme, covering different topics in due course. It may be the church's life one week, the education system another, or crime and the police, prisons another week, the economy another week, and then leadership in church and country. The media and the entertainment sector are in great need of prayer because they are so influential, and of course many churches will want to cry out to God for revival. Congregational prayer like this, perhaps carried out for six months, seems to make a remarkable difference to the spiritual climate of a church.

Prayer Triplets were happening, I fancy, in England before they ever reached Singapore. I recall the way they were introduced to prepare the way for one of Billy Graham's visits to this country. I am told some 18,000 people came to Christ during the preparatory year in which these groups were operating. The idea is very simple. Three people, usually friends, covenant to get together regularly once a week and pray for three friends each who are not yet Christians. Jesus promised great things to the 'two or three' gathered to pray in his name, and it is not long before results are seen. Of course, the focus can change. It need not always concern your three friends and those of your colleagues. It could be prayer for spiritual awakening, or for some particular project. It is important not to allow this to become merely a time of social chit-chat and maybe a meal. Though these may feature when the friends meet together, the purpose is prayer and that must have the priority. Lives are full, and it is important to find a time and place people are comfortable with and to stick to an agreed timing for the meeting. Fortunate is the church that is honeycombed with such triplets. They can undergird the whole work and outreach of the church, and are utterly informal and flexible.

2. Profiling

This is simply the necessary work of getting to know your chosen area, not as it appears to be but as it really is. They do it so that they can understand the community better and express love more deeply and appropriately. We in the West attempt something similar in the 'audit' which some churches carry out for their territory. There are several obvious benefits in doing this. For one thing, it enables you to get to know your community, and to get known yourself. For another it is likely to suggest ways in which, in due course, that community can be penetrated for Christ. And in the meantime it provides much fuel for prayer as you become acquainted with some of the real life situations there.

Singapore churches do this in a very intentional way. They

generally start with library research on the area, if any exists. They move on to face-to-face casual contacts, by means of a short conversation when distributing small gifts such as mandarin oranges at Chinese New Year. They record what they have found out and build on it in subsequent visits. They later conduct a comprehensive survey through carefully designed questionnaires. Collating the information thus gleaned, they begin to build up a composite picture of the block of flats or area. It becomes plain what are the dominant mindsets, the main problems and anxieties of the community, and what is the spiritual climate of the place. Some of these questionnaires are designed for shops, others for residents. The most fruitful are enquiries about what are the perceived needs in the community. Often in-depth interviews emerge, and friendships are forged. Meanwhile the church begins to get a coherent idea of how best to penetrate into the community with the gospel. Some churches wisely take round postcards beforehand to inform the residents that they will be conducting a survey on such and such a day. They print the survey in the variety of languages needed in the area, usually English, Malay, Chinese and Tamil. The results are entered on a database, and intense prayer is undertaken before they decide on and adopt the next phase in this operation of displaying God's love. One church found that many of the locals were only just surviving, and so they found ways of making them gifts. Chinese people love 'ang pows' during Chinese New Year, and that proves to be a very acceptable way in. There is a 'mooncake festival' in September, and that furnishes an obvious opportunity for gifts of cake, but they also dream up primary English and Maths classes, a concert, or whatever seems to be called for as a result of the survey.

3. Projects

The ideals these Singaporean Christians set before themselves are those of Jesus the Servant. But they see this servant ministry in two slightly different ways, which they call *Kindness*

Projects and *Penetration Programmes*. The former are under-taken to change people's perception of the church. Thus acts of kindness, with no strings attached, can be very effective in bringing about a change in the church's image. Penetration programmes are carried out with the specific aim of opening people's hearts to the Christians and their gospel. In kindness projects the contact is often momentary: it is a one-off without follow-up, task-oriented, making use of the element of surprise. It involves the church going to the community, embodies kindness and can take place before any profiling is done. On the other hand penetration programmes are designed to open hearts to Christians, and to build relation-ships. They connect repeatedly with the same people, and so it is an ongoing affair. Conscious efforts are made to follow up, and often members of the community are invited to some aspect of the church's programme that may be appropriate for them.

Kindness Projects

Some kindness projects that I came across were the following. Free Christmas gift-wrap at a shopping mall (by agreement, of course, with the management). This is designed simply to be an unexpected blessing to the shoppers and also to build relationships with the mall owners. They have printed a small card to attach to the purchase, once they have wrapped it: 'Showing you God's love in a practical way'. This fascinates the shoppers – and indeed the mall owners. Sometimes so much so that they pay for the wrapping paper and ribbon. Otherwise the church does.

Another fascinating initiative is to offer a free taxi wash and vacuum. A few days prior to the event, Christians go to the cafés where taxi drivers are known to congregate, and tell them what is on offer. They borrow or purchase the nec-essary cleaning equipment, and often they operate a 'coffee corner' to warm the taxi drivers as they wait. Then they give them the little card, 'Showing you God's love in a practical way', and the amazed taxi drivers go on their way – thinking furiously!

Incidentally, I was delighted to hear from the assistant bishop of West Malaysia that they have adopted a similar project there, 'Love Malaysia'. Christians offer to wash taxis just as they do in Singapore. And Christian taxi drivers are famous for their courtesy and the trouble they go to in order to return anything left in their taxi to the rightful owners. The newspapers have noticed it! Two similar projects are offering to wash a neighbourhood hair salon and a neighbourhood coffee shop. They negotiate with local government to remove bulky items that people in the area want to get rid of. They inform the locals of this service and the day on which it will happen. The better stuff they take to the Salvation Army and Thrift Shops for recycling, the rest they dispose of in the local rubbish dumps. Simple and amazing. It will only take two or three hours, but the impression made will long outlast that.

There are other projects, such as the distribution of 'goodies' to elderly residents in the neighbourhood, or something similar in the local school.

One can never move from one culture to another without adaptation. Some of the practical expedients adopted in Singapore would make a Londoner cringe. But the principle of practical kindness without strings attached lies very near the heart of the gospel. We must try to find culturally appropriate ways of embodying that principle. We need to overflow with grace! I recall an occasion when some of us took a tray of Mars bars into the street and offered them free to passers-by, with a printed inscription 'Free, just like God's love'. This provides a variety of responses. Often people are highly suspicious. Often they want to pay for them! Sometimes we have run a dinner for street people, for the police or the teachers – a sort of 'We appreciate you' event. This is not what they expect of the church, and it has a considerable impact and gives good contacts to follow through. Yes, these things do happen in England – a little.

But we have a long way to go before we match the deliberate kindness outreach which marks evangelism in Singapore and which is such a lovely expression of God's generosity to human beings without a word needing to be said!

Penetration Programmes

The aim here is to make their presence felt in the neighbourhood with a view to building relationships and developing them in the cause of the gospel. These are some of the ways they go about it.

A number of them are very familiar to us, because much the same approaches are adopted in Britain. We know about School Assembly work, Holiday Camps, Study Programmes, and Children's Church. But we rarely do anything comparable to Block Parties. The Singaporeans put these on in a neutral spot near the high-rise block. It might be a hamburger party, a children's art competition and tea party, Tutti Frutti, Mooncake party and so forth. The theme determines the decoration, songs, games and activities. All is carefully prepared. The date is fixed and publicized well in advance, on a school or public holiday. They aim for about fifty at a time, enough to make a splash, and not so many that it is impossible to spend time with individuals. Flyers are prepared and distributed in the block, and the volunteers give themselves to prayer. A variation on this is a Kids' Club. Once again the careful preparation, publicity and prayer. They set up a database of those who come. They send them a letter afterwards, inviting them to a future event. They write to individuals at least once a quarter. They make available a weekly drop-in with games, help on studies, craft work and so forth during school term. Before long, excellent relationships are established that may well in due time lead these youngsters into conversion and discipleship. Sometimes churches go to the effort of putting on a personal tuition scheme in this land where education is everything. Once again comes the survey to see what is needed, once again the publicity to make known the offer, once again the intentional and prevailing prayer. They mobilize volunteer tutors, monitor progress and keep parents informed. This is enormously appreciated and gives a wonderful demonstration of the caring nature of the local Christian community. Naturally a weekend sports activity for young people is a powerful draw, as it is in the West. But they also come up with an appreciation dinner for mothers and fathers in the community, combined with a concert. No effort is spared to demonstrate the practical love of God.

At times they progress to a larger event, and if the preparation hitherto has gone well, it will be a big draw. One of the local churches has found a locality musical event to be very effective. The unique thing about it is that the whole church is mobilized to take part in the operation, perhaps in the cast, or as an intercessor, an usher or a distributor of flyers to every flat in the area. Others serve by offering hospitality and engaging in conversation after the event. When a couple of these musicals have taken place it is safe to put out a response slip at the next event, to see who among the audience would like to take things further on the Christian front. And this has all been achieved without putting the rest of the people off: they have learned to trust these Christians with their acts of kindness.

The Singaporeans have realized that 'evangelism' is a scary word to Christians and non-Christians alike. Christians are hesitant about it through past experience, embarrassment, ignorance of what to say, and fear of failure. In traditional verbal-based evangelism we Christians use the power of words and arguments to try to help others to faith. And because we feel we could never do it well enough, most of us do not even try. With kindness evangelism, however, they use the power of God's love and generosity to attract people to Christ. And that is not threatening, either to them or to the recipients. They have discovered that it is a 'low risk – high grace' path to outreach. Like their English cousins, they are well aware that God's kindness comes to us through an extended *process*, and that only when we know we are accepted do we feel liberated and able to respond. They even have a little mnemonic, an ABC to help them. *Ask* God to show you the needs and difficulties of those around you. *Be* practical in responding to them: actions need to precede words. And *Commit* yourself to action. There is an old saying of C. H. Spurgeon that they love: 'Be good, get good, and do good. Do all the good you can; to all the people that you can; and as long as you can.'

Most recently 'Love Singapore' has been promoting a 'seven wave harvest', brilliantly set out in an outstanding media campaign. Sabah is following suit in a 'Love KK' campaign.

What a powerful approach! We could readily devise various other ways to show kindness within our culture to the people in a chosen territorial area. That is not a problem. The approach is basically simple. But my questions are these. Do we, like them, believe that the gospel is vital for everyone? Do we share their passion for lost people? Do we have their commitment to get involved in the needs of strangers? Do we have the perseverance? Do we know anything about that sort of prevailing prayer? Are we prepared to face the cost, in terms of time, money and commitment?

4. Partnership

For all their geographical proximity in a small island, they realize that no one church and no one type of approach will be able to reach the whole of Singapore. The vision is crystal clear: to turn Singapore towards the living God. But any vision will remain wishful thinking if it is not allied to a strategy. And that strategy is what they call 'geo-networks'. This is simply a fancy way of carving up the territory in the island – that is the easy part. And then getting all the churches in that area to work together – that is the difficult part. But they have set their sights on nothing less. They know, from our Lord's prayer in John 17, that unity is essential for mission. They know there is no point in duplicating precious effort and resources. They know that the approach of one church will not necessarily sit comfortably with another. They know that it takes all the churches in an area to affect that neighbourhood for Christ. So they take very seriously the principle of partnership in mission.

They go about it wisely. They know that every church likes to run things in its own way, and that no church likes to be organized and told what to do by others. So they respect this. They affirm the unique contribution of each church. But they strive to create a partnership which is loose in structure but strong in relationship. They are careful to help every church to see how their own agenda can be furthered by being part of the geo-network. They never introduce anything that would make a church less effective or cause it to give up some cherished area of investment. They do not have many meetings, knowing how busy pastors are and how they dislike going to endless committees. But they ensure that every moment counts in the meetings they do have. So relationships build up, vision is enhanced, and confidence grows. And they wisely continue to affirm churches which decide not to be part of the network. As a result a good few of them join in later on.

The aim of the geo-network is clear: to reach out to lost people with the gospel. The methods are varied. The partnership is enriching. The strategies develop as the relationships are strengthened. Dividing up the area is a ticklish business and calls for a lot of tact – which is not always in evidence. So let us not imagine that Singapore has got it all right. At times they are quarrelsome, at times abrasive, at times discouraged. After all, Singapore is a massive, multicultural, materialistic culture which the church has not yet been able to penetrate effectively. But the churches have grasped the importance of a shared vision. They have grasped the importance of partnership instead of isolationism or competition. They have grasped the importance of recognizing and rejoicing in each other's strengths, and they even see their different ways of doing things as an enrichment of the Christian tapestry in the island.

Surely this is a vital lesson for us. I think of a recent mission in a great British city, involving scores of churches. Several teams were used in this mission. And the team where I was involved failed to reach its potential. Not because of poor planning: it was excellent. Not because of failure in prayer: that was unremitting. But because the churches did not get their act together. There was not that love and partnership, that mutual trust and common vision, that are needed if the great task of evangelization is to take place.

On the other hand I think of a great city overseas where I led a mission some years ago, with a medium-sized team. It was not well organized: in fact the local organization was rather chaotic. But there was tremendous fruit. We had the privilege of bumping into complete strangers in the streets, belonging to different ethnic groups, who were hungry for God. We had the joy of leading them to Christ and launching them on a life of discipleship. What, under God, was the secret? I think it was that the ministers had met together weekly for some seven years. They had prayed together for the city for an hour or so, eaten a bag lunch and gone home. They made that Wednesday prayer time a top priority. Each of them had, at some time on one of these Wednesdays, confessed his weaknesses and indeed wept before his brothers. It was that bonding among the leadership, that desire not to further their own petty empires but the great Kingdom of God, together with their love and prayer – *that* is what had prepared the ground for what became rather a remarkable mission. And that is a lesson which Singapore is superbly placed to teach us, from their own deep mutual commitment and effective practical achievements.

As I reflect on the leadership of our Western churches, it seems to me that many are not leaders. Even more seriously, some of them appear to have no living relationship with Christ. I am not looking for a crisis conversion, but for evidence of spiritual life, whatever the person's churchmanship.

Without a personal relationship with Christ it is impossible to lead anyone else to him. Many churches, many clergy do not even try. They seem content with the usually smallish numbers who attend church, and make no serious effort to win the unconverted. Even at the end of the Decade of Evangelism you find many churches very timid about any form of outreach. On a mission in a large city recently, a mission which the city had asked for, our team were repeatedly asked not to mention Jesus Christ when we talked with people!

That is what our friends in South East Asia cannot understand. It is simply beyond their comprehension, as one of them put it to me recently, why we are so timid, so lacking in confidence about our faith and so lax in attempting to spread it. But of course it comes down to a matter of leadership. I am amused to recall my first meeting with the undergraduate body attached to the church, when I was appointed rector of St Aldate's, Oxford. I suggested, at the end of the evening, that we should do some outdoor ministry in the street just outside the church the next day, which was a Saturday. The self-appointed leader of the group said to me, 'We do not do that sort of thing here.' I looked him in the eye and said, 'Maybe we don't. But we are going to do it tomorrow, and what is more you are going to be there, taking part!' He was, and he is now ordained. That seemed to me a critical moment when leadership was called for. We in the West are in sore need of clergy who are leaders, and thankfully, leadership is one of the areas where this young Province can give us some helpful suggestions.

3

Learning about the Cell Church

It would not be possible to carry out a fraction of the ministry of kindness which we have been considering in the last chapter were it not for the small cells into which most of the churches are subdivided. Indeed, it would be more accurate to say that the cell church is the basic unit, and that the 'churches' as we know them are an aggregate of cells, which meet on a Sunday for the purposes of celebration. Arguable though it may be, for them the cell is the basic Christian community.

One of the most remarkable Anglican cell churches I know is St Patrick's, Tawau, in Sabah, that part of East Malaysia which used to be known as British North Borneo. The priest is Archdeacon Albert Vun, and he presides over a rapidly growing church. When he took it over a few years ago, it was a fairly large and normal Anglican congregation with 500 or so adherents. Now it is over 3,000 and has no fewer than 315 cells – and the number is increasing all the time. He gave an electrifying address at the 1999 Anglican Church Leaders Conference in Singapore, and I am indebted to him for much of what follows.

At the very outset he put his finger, with wit and charm, on two of the great weaknesses of the Western church, without even mentioning us! He began with God's promise to Abraham, that 'in you all the families of the earth shall be blessed' (Genesis 12.3) and showed how that prophecy was meant to be fulfilled through the church: 'so you see, those who believe are the descendants of Abraham' (Galatians 3.7). The church was meant to be fruitful in outreach to the world. That was the main point of Jesus' analogy of the vine and its branches. Some branches bear no fruit: they are use-less and are burnt. Some bear a modicum of fruit: these are carefully pruned. The aim of the gardener is to have much fruit, and it is the contention of these Christian leaders in South East Asia that the cell church is the most effective way to bear much fruit for God. Results seem to bear them out. In this striking opening of his address Albert brought home to the delegates the divine imperative to grow and multi-ply – the very thing that embarrasses us so much in the West, because most of us are shrinking rather than growing.

The second area on which he placed an unerring finger was the traditional way of 'doing church'. Of course, Robert Warren has drawn our attention in Britain to the contrast between the traditional and the emerging church. But change is slow. We are trapped by our past, and believe instinctively that there is only one proper way of being the church, espe-cially the Anglican Church, and that is by behaving much as we have traditionally behaved. Albert asked people to reflect why the Church of St Michael, Sandakan (in Sabah) was built with a sharply sloping roof. The answer was 'to enable the snow to slide down easily'. Of course there has never been any snow in Sandakan, though there was plenty in Western Europe where this type of church roof was designed! Naturally, this sally brought waves of laughter. But he made his point. People think the church lives in the past and is bound by the past, inherited way of doing things. They do not believe we have relevance to the present or hope for the future. That is where the cell church can help us.

What is a cell church?

1. It is a grouping of vibrant and multiplying communities of believers.
2. Every cell is seen as a church, set in its neighbourhood to impact it.
3. Every cell leader is a pastor, who always has an assistant.
4. The cell consists of between about seven and 15 people.
5. When it exceeds about 15 the cell multiplies into two, the assistant leader assuming the leadership of the new cell.

6. Cells can be of many sorts. You can have children's cells, youth cells, cells for business people, homemakers, nurses. Or you can have the normal cross-section of society making up the cell. Usually they come from a common location – homes, hospital, school, business, army camps, etc. There is nothing randomly iconoclastic about all this. It is not change for the sake of change. It is change in pursuit of vision, the vision of building a great network of flexible, Christ-centred and Spirit-filled communities which seek God's way to meet human need throughout Singapore, Sabah and beyond. That is the vision. The goal that they currently have in Singapore is to establish a home cell in every street in the city. And the strategy is simple: multiply cells out of the existing ones, particularly in a chosen area or territory. In England this might most naturally be a parish.

What is the ethos of a cell church?

In Britain many churches have Bible study groups. That is not the purpose of the cell, though Bible study may well form a part of the programme at times. The fastest growing cell church in West Malaysia does not allow Bibles in the cell meetings – too threatening for newcomers! Nor is it primarily a group for prayer. It is a group of Christians meeting for fellowship and service, and their shepherd is the cell leader. They like to summarize the purpose of the cell as twofold: edification (building up one another in love) and multiplication (building up the cell by loving others outside it and welcoming them in). They sometimes summarize its purpose with three Ms.

- Ministry to God through praise and worship.
- Ministry to each other through Scripture, spiritual gifts, practical help, counselling and prayer – all held together with activities which increase bonding.
- Ministry to the world through a Christian lifestyle,

verbal witness to Christ, adopting and praying for a
missionary, and going on short-term mission trips.

One can immediately see the advantages of such a way of
'doing church'. It minimizes church organizations, while
maximizing community and ministry. It equips and mobilizes
the whole church, since everybody is a member of a cell. It
enhances the whole concept of the pilgrim status of the
church, since it is always in transition. It is highly flexible and
does not require any property other than a home. It promotes
accountability and minimizes the temptation to be dependent
on church buildings.

Is the cell church effective?

It is effective in a number of ways.

1. In the first place, it is effective for *community*.

It is people-based, not programme-based. Albert recounted
amusingly how his Tawau church had endless committees
when he took over – and he was expected to be at all of them.
The church grew – and so did the committees, and the
exhaustion. Many of the committees were useless for advanc-
ing the work of God: they consisted of the unqualified, drawn
from the unwilling, to do the unnecessary! God founded a
family, not a committee. Relationship is more important than
organization. That is a vital principle of church life.

Nowadays in Tawau only eight hours a year are taken up
with committees: the PCC meets four times for two hours!
They perceive that committee work kills relations with non-
Christians. It makes for salt that has lost its savour and never
gets out as a preservative among the meat. Jesus did not
operate by committee! And so now Tawau church has at least
145 adult cells, 105 children cell groups and 65 for youth.
That has certainly made a massive difference to the sense of
community in the church. It presents a big contrast to our
somewhat ineffective committee-bound way of doing things.

2. Cell churches can also be much more effective for *pastoral care*.

Numerous studies have shown that no one clergyman can effectively act as a pastor to a church of more than 150 or at the most 200. It reaches a plateau at that stage under single leadership, however gifted the pastor. But with this cell system where the pastoral work is entrusted to the leader of the small cell, the sky is the limit. Since adopting cell church principles in 1990, the numbers at Vun's church have consistently risen. The average Sunday attendance was 600 in 1990, 796 in 1991, 1,038 in 1994, 1,536 in 1997, 2,800 in November 1999, and by February 2000 well over 3,000. They would not come if they were not pastored and cared for! The largest church in the world, that of Yonggi Cho in South Korea, which has well in excess of 10,000 members, is broken down into cells of a dozen or so, where the discipling is done and the growth occurs.

3. The cell church is effective for *church growth*.

Tawau is an interesting example of a common trend wherever the cell is adopted as the basic unit of church life. In 1995, for example, they had 608 professions of conversion, in 1997 1,021, and in 1998 1,400. With non-Western expectancy and precision, they set an evangelistic goal each year for the church at large and for each cell. Baptisms are normally by immersion on a Saturday, not in a church building but in a populous place, so that the vitality of the church is evident to passers-by. Many of these are children and young people. The church is careful to see that it does not spend so much time looking after the old that it fails to connect with the rising generation. That too is an important lesson which we in the West have failed to learn.

4. The cell church is also effective for *spiritual ministry*.

They take seriously the teaching of 1 Corinthians 12 that there are a variety of ministries given to God's people by the Holy Spirit. These are intended for the common good and for building up the whole Christian community. For there is no such thing as a Christian who does not have a ministry. Moreover, they take seriously the teaching of Ephesians 4 that what we might call the 'ordained ministry' of apostle, prophet, evangelist, teacher and pastor, exists for the purpose of equipping other members of Christ's body so that each limb can play its part effectively. Consequently, in Tawau they do not make the mistake of restricting the idea of 'ministry' to what is done publicly by the vicar in church on Sunday. It is exercised all over the place by the members of the cells. In our traditional churches we often fail to empower the laity. Clergy can discourage ministry among members of the congregation by taking too much of it upon themselves. Indeed, we do not generally have the structures to enable people to discover and exercise their God-given gifts in ministry. But the cell church makes that very easy.

I had a marvellous object lesson in that area on one visit to Tawau. Albert told me they were having a big celebratory dinner at which I was to speak evangelistically. He told me that there would be 450 there, half of whom were church members and the other half not yet Christians, but close friends of the cell members. He asked me not to ask for any sign of response at the end, but to leave that to the cell members. I confess that I thought that risky, but I learnt an invaluable lesson that night. My wife and I were staying with Albert, and his phone kept ringing with news from one church member after another that their friend, present at the dinner, had committed themselves to Christ. It was they who had befriended that person in the first place. They had taken him or her to the dinner. And it was they who had the privilege of bringing to birth the new believer. Entirely appropriate. Albert had done the work he was ordained to do. He had built up the saints for the work of ministry (Ephesians 4.11) and we could all see the fruitfulness of it. And of course, if government pressure were to close churches, as it might in many countries and did in Russia, China and Eastern Germany, these churches would survive, since they consist of lots of small cells, meeting at unpredictable hours

in private homes under lay leadership. Under such circumstances the cell church would not only be very effective for
spiritual ministry. It would survive, and probably grow – in a
way the traditional church assuredly would not.

5. The cell church is also very effective for *the nurture
   of new Christians.*

You do not need to keep running centralized courses for new
believers, with all the evident disadvantages of rupture when
the course ends, because the nurture is done in the place where
the initial contact and the conversion took place, the cell. The
quality of instruction may not be so high, but the power of
example, the proximity of other believers and the passion to
multiply are all major advantages. I noticed among the
Pentecostals in Chile that new converts were ushered at once
into small home groups whose aim was to nurture, to witness, to edify one another and to multiply. In South East
Asia, as in the UK, there are lots of emotionally and physi-
cally abused children. They may well have no model to follow
at home, but in the cell they get love, discipline and a sense
of belonging. It is a highly effective environment for nurture.

6. The cell church method is also very useful for
   broadening the leadership base.

In almost any traditional church there is a desperate shortage
of leaders. Here, leaders emerge in abundance. The advantages
are obvious. One-man ministry is limited in reach: this
spreads widely. One-man ministry is limited in time: this
enlarges it. One-man ministry is limited in impact: through
cell leaders it is greatly extended. One person finds it very
hard to mobilize a church; there are many drones in the
hive. But when the cell leader gets to work on his group of
twelve or so, it is hard for the idle to lie low! Cell leadership
facilitates maximum involvement and gets the church active.
The broadening of the leadership at Tawau is very sugges-
tive. In 1992 they had 23 cells, trained no leaders, and cell
attendance was 305. In 1995 they had 118 cells, trained 250
leaders and cell attendance was 771. In 1999 they had 330

cells, trained upwards of 700 leaders, and had a cell attendance of 3,100. Those figures speak for themselves. There is
a very broad leadership cadre for Christ's work in and
through that church.

7. Cell churches are effective for *rapid churchplanting*.

And that is an area where we in the West are weak. It was
fascinating to hear from a young man still in his twenties. He
had gone from Tawau to West Malaysia, and, with the
goodwill of their bishop, had set about planting an Anglican
church in Kuala Lumpur. He began with six people four
years ago. They were young people like himself, and met as
a cell on a weekday evening in a house. They decided to move
it to Sunday, still with six people. In April 1995 they were
eight, and then increased to fifteen, and then to thirty. People
were sitting up the stairs and in the kitchen. So they moved
to a bigger place. Now they number fifty, and are broken
down into four cell groups. Their PCC is made up of people
approximately 22 years old!

Their passion to grow is exemplary. One of their cells was
made up of teenagers. They walked around the area, praying
for it, on six Sunday afternoons. On the sixth week they also
leafleted all the homes for any young people who would like
to know more about Jesus. Next week they waited anxiously,
and only one girl came along. They were discouraged, but to
their amazement five minutes later about 70 rolled up! Kids
bring kids, and the thing grows. Now they number about
170 on a Sunday, and of course they have their weeknight
cells as well. And all that through a single youngster with a
heart for God and the training he has received in Tawau. He
remarked modestly, 'Two is enough to start a cell.' It certainly
is, and if so, what is stopping us in the West from doing like-
wise?

I recall an Anglican house church in Santiago. It all began
with one man singing hymns and choruses with his guitar,
under a tree in a small residential square. He was entirely on
his own, and did it every week. Eventually someone took pity
on him and stood with him. And so it began. The time I

visited it, there were about 30 young people and about 40 others all crammed into the house and small garden, enjoying each other's company, eating breakfast, and in due course dividing into two groups for appropriate worship. It left an indelible impression upon me. I have little doubt that this is the way for the church to advance in the twenty-first century, when informality is going to be the key, relationships are going to be crucial, and tradition and hierarchy are going to be at a discount. There is no doubt that the cell church is effective.

Can cell churches be Anglican?

I hope readers who are not Anglicans will allow this question and indeed interpret it in terms of their own denominational structure. I refer to Anglicans here not only because the cell churches I have examined are in fact Anglican, but also because the cell church as such would seem sharply to contradict the Anglican emphasis on bishops, presbyters and deacons as the ordained ministry of the church. Clearly, therefore, it is an important issue for Anglicans and other mainline churches.

Most of the cell churches in the world probably belong to independent structures. The movement has received enormous encouragement and training from Ralph W. Neighbour, who hails from the Navigators. He and his friend Lawrence Khong launched a cell church in Singapore which in seven years passed the 7,000 mark. But it is not Anglican. Is this a way of being the church that is possible for Anglicans and other mainline churches?

The answer is yes, but it is a costly yes.

First, it is going to mean getting the approval of the bishop. He may well regard it as a risky and almost maverick procedure. In Sabah there is a great man as a bishop, who at the time of writing has just become archbishop of the Province. He is happy to give his backing to Albert Vun, and willing to endure the angry letters that come from some of the parishioners. Moreover, with a brilliant exhibition of leadership, he takes Albert Vun and makes him an archdeacon. That is to

say, he takes what could be regarded as a dangerous initiator
and brings him into the heart of the establishment. But not all
bishops have the courage and vision to do something like
that. And without episcopal approval it is difficult to see how
an Anglican church could move over to a cell church model.

For make no mistake about it, this is a total move. Away
goes the Men's Group and the Mothers Union, the Flower
Guild and the Boy's Brigade. All the organizations disappear
at one fell swoop. You can either run a traditional church
with all the accompanying organizations that we are familiar
with, or a cell church, where all activity goes on in the cells.
What you cannot do is to combine both. A cell church is not
like a home group, which many churches in the West have
tried, and largely given up on! It is the focus for one's Christian
life. It is the instrument of nurture and training; the instrument, too, of evangelization and service. You can't do a 'both
and'. You have to go for an 'either or'. And that is very costly
to the congregation, especially to the die-hards. It is very
challenging to the vicar because his time will almost totally
be taken up with training: training the lay pastors to whom
much of his leadership is to be deputed. Many clergy do not
see this equipping as their calling, nor, indeed, do they have
the talent and training for it. It will require setting goals, and
thoughtfully reaching out in evangelism and service to the
community. It will require accountability. And all this is
rather threatening to many a vicar.

There are two important areas in the cell church philosophy
which present serious difficulties for Anglicans. The first is
the tendency to see the cell leader as the pastor. This could be
seen to demean the role of the parish priest. But this need not
be so at all. Just as the bishop shares his territorial oversight
with the priest, a 'cure both thine and mine', so the parish
priest shares that same oversight with his lay pastors who
look after the cells. In both cases it is a matter of general
responsibility and delegated oversight. And the cell leader has
no more right to go off in his own direction regardless of
the vicar, than the vicar has regardless of the bishop.

The other delicate area concerns who may celebrate the

Holy Communion. In many other denominations, and non-denominational organizations like the Navigators, this presents no problem. They are not fussy who breaks bread. But in the Anglican, Presbyterian, Baptist, Roman and Orthodox communions there is a strict rule of consecration by a priest or ordained minister. There are many within the Anglican Communion who chafe at this, particularly those who belong to the evangelical wing of the church. However, that is the rule, and in Britain at least, it brooks no exceptions. And if you are going to see as your main pastor the cell leader, what are you going to do about baptism and the eucharist?

However, there is no insuperable problem here. Let the main celebratory gathering of the whole church on a Sunday be eucharistic, either regularly each week or less frequently. The act of consecration will appropriately be led by the priest. If the cell church wants to break bread together there are various ways of handling this. One is to invite the vicar to come and share in the evening and then to conduct a simple communion service. Another is to use elements that have previously been consecrated in church: this expedient is likely to appeal to those of a Catholic disposition. Those whose instincts are more evangelical may well have recourse to a simple *agape*. This is a 'love feast' and used to accompany the Holy Communion in the early days of Christianity. It has been revived in several circles these days, and is basically a community meal within the group or cell, with varied contents: a meal, praise, prayer, testimony, and at some point in the evening a simple breaking of break and sharing wine in remembrance of Jesus. This is done without any words of consecration, without robes or books: it is totally informal, and if properly safeguarded, it does not break canon law and is no threat to Anglican order.

So far as I can see, therefore, there is no insuperable problem in having Anglican churches organized on this cell church model. However, there are important issues which must be faced. It can hardly be denied that most advance in Christianity down the centuries has come from below, not by imposition from above. And the cell church model is heavily

dominated by the church's top leadership who set the goals
and require the compliance. This is a genuine danger which
requires watching.

What is needed in a lively cell?

The most important element in a cell is the vision, quality
and commitment of the leadership. Without that, nothing
effective happens. It is crucial to have leaders who do not
merely facilitate the gifts of others but are active in leadership
themselves. This seems to be an area where the churches of
the Province have been particularly successful, and we shall
be looking at the whole question of leadership in a subsequent
chapter.

But granted the crucial importance of the leader, the group
must have a clear vision of what they are about, and that
vision is determined by the goals of the church as a whole.
There is no hope of success if the part has a different aim
from the whole. That is why leadership needs to be strong.
Sometimes church people rather like weak pastors who make
no demands on them and let them go the way they want. But
Singaporean Christians are very impressed by the leadership
which Lee Kuan Yew has offered to the country at large. It is
firm, consistent and unwavering. Not everybody likes it, but
everybody knows where they stand with it. And so it is with
the cell groups. They have leaders who seek to inculcate in
the cell the vision that drives the whole church.

All too often the direction of a body of people is confused
because there are too many aims. In the effective cell there are
only two, and the leader keeps them before the eyes of all.
One is to minister, and the other is to multiply. To love one
another inside the cell, and to love others outside the cell.
This is not only clear: it is revolutionary. For it is nothing
less than the 'new commandment' that lies at the heart of
Jesus' ethics. In church life in the West it is often given nom-
inal approval but no explicit action. In South East Asia it
determines everything. Thus within the group they set out to
meet the needs of each other. They ask how the day has gone

for each member, what they have each been learning from God and through the Scriptures and experience. What problems have been encountered? What needs crush the members? And these are lovingly prayed over, and if practical help is called for, the cell provides it. This could, and often does include financial help if a brother or sister becomes unemployed. It is love in action. And people invited in as the friends of members sense this love and mutual caring. It is so unlike anything they have met elsewhere. It is very attractive, and it predisposes them to want to find out more.

There is a rough pattern which is regularly followed in the cell meeting: Welcome, Worship, Warmth, Word, Works. After an enthusiastic welcome all round, the evening begins with an 'ice-breaker', usually an imaginative game which involves some physical movement and in which everybody takes part. This helps to put people at their ease, bond people together and underline the fact that there are no passengers in the cell. I asked some of the leaders in the Province just how important this ice-breaker is, because in Britain initial games can seem rather juvenile and off-putting. The answer was instructive. The use of an ice-breaker starts the meeting with an emphasis on human interaction. If we cannot relate to each other, it will not be easy to relate to God. So the ice-breaker, whether it takes the form of humour, a game, or whatever, helps to break down our barriers and inhibitions and to focus the group on each other as a family and God as the heavenly Father. Ice-breakers are all about helping people to relax and relate. They believe that if you cannot build those basic relationships in a small group, you cannot build the church of God.

If someone has a birthday or it is some other special occasion, then that is given prominence. A time of loud and joyful praise to God will normally follow. That leads into prayer. Subsequently the leader draws out members of the cell to make their own contributions to the life of the cell. The place of testimony is highly valued (see Revelation 12.11). Everyone is encouraged to share how their Christian life is going, and what God has taught them in the past week.

A short talk invariably follows. It is given by the leader, and generally takes home and applies what was taught from the pulpit on Sunday. In this way the cell leaders reinforce the pastor's teaching and apply it practically to daily life. There is opportunity for questions and discussion to follow. And there will follow a closing hymn before a time of ministry, in which everyone is encouraged and personally prayed for. Everybody is important. The ministry is not always exercised by the leader. Someone else may have a vision or a gift of healing that may be called for. In this way the cell members are put together again after the hassles of the week. They are loved, taught, encouraged and ministered to. They have opportunity to sing, pray, discuss and give their testimony. It is a healthy balance. And before they leave they decide what practical action they will take as a group. Much was said about that in the previous chapter. The whole thing lasts an hour and a half. And regular attendance is very important. That is how people sense their unity in Christ, and grow in love, understanding and service.

That is only the merest outline. Newcomers change the dynamics of the group, and an evening with newcomers will need to be sensitively handled. New believers grow by osmosis into the group, and are catered for by one of the group's members in one-on-one pastoral care. Failing that, the church will have regular back-up groups for nurture. The Singaporeans and Sabahans are very practical about it all. If parents have very young children, the father and mother may be asked to belong to different cells so that there is someone at home to look after the babies without the expense of a babysitter. Confidentiality is very important in these cells where people open so much of their lives to one another. And so is in-service training for the leaders. There is in fact, as we shall see in a subsequent chapter, a whole net-work of cell supervisors, so that no leader has to battle on alone. A supervisor will look after the leaders of several cells, and will call them from time to time for a lunchtime meeting, lasting no more than an hour, which will encourage them and help them sort out problems.

How do cells multiply?

The multiplication of cells is a major aim, and it is sustained. People rarely stay in a cell for more than six or nine months. In that time it will have grown and split. If not, the cell is closed! They have no room for dysfunctional cells of lazy or disaffected members.

Of course, multiplication and evangelism go hand in hand. The cell churches realize, shrewdly, that building-centred evangelism is not really ideal if you want to involve the whole people of God. There the clergy do all the important stuff. It is they who devise the programmes, lead the services and preach. And the laity accept it, enthusiastically or passively. But with cell-based evangelism it is very different. Every new Christian is expected to win one other person to Christ within a year or two. He does not preach to his friend. He just invites him or her into the cell. And because the cell is set in the community and is indeed part of the community, it is a non-threatening environment for the friend to be invited to. It does not involve alien customs, dress and liturgy (no liturgy is used in the cells). It is Christ-centred, lively, loving and fairly natural. Very often the newcomer comes again next week, and is soon a committed follower of Christ, ready to be built up in the cell and then to go out with friends in the cell for the acts of kindness and community penetration outlined in the previous chapter.

Much is made of the parable of the Great Supper in Luke 14, where the master of the feast is very concerned that his house should be full. The servants are sent out to invite people in. Further, they bring them in – they are accompanied. If that fails, 'Make them come in!' says the Master. And they do! They use a lot of persuasion to get their friends to come to the cell, 'so that my house may be full'.

There is a passion about these Far Eastern Christians which is most disturbing: it convicts me of my coldness of heart and half-heartedness in the work of evangelism. They have another of their favourite acronyms, PUSH. Pray Until Salvation Happens!

In this way the cells grow, and when they reach about fifteen they split into two halves, with the assistant leader taking half the group off so that both halves can repeat the process and reach out afresh. Leaders commit themselves very seriously and long-term to the task of pastoring a group. They do not want the members to say, 'Our pastor dies every three years!' They are there for the long haul. Cell leadership is the basic building-block of the church.

This being the case, it is not surprising that the cells are very intentional about the whole multiplication process. Having set a date to split and multiply, they work hard to bring that about. Part of the leader's responsibility is to maintain that vision among his cell members. They make it a major item of prayer, individually and in the cell. They train an intern leader, in expectation of his or her being needed very soon. They go all out to find and invite new members, win them and nurture them. The outreach is very Singaporean – many Westerners would call it aggressive. They would not mind the description, but regard it as a compliment.

One of the ways of multiplication which they particularly enjoy is some occasion for celebration. People love food in Singapore, and you can draw all sorts of people to a good dinner. So these dinners take place quite often, and are wonderful occasions to bring new people and thereafter to draw them into your cell. These feasts can be at the level of a cell, a cluster of cells, a zone, or a townwide occasion. Just as the Alpha course has found food to be such a vital ingredient, so has the outreach of the East. There is a special relationship that emerges when you go to a good dinner with other people. Perhaps that is why our Lord did not leave us a book or a set of instructions, but a meal!

How do you effect transition to a cell church?

This may well be a crucial question for some readers, and it certainly was for some of the Asian leaders who now lead flourishing cell churches. The received wisdom is to start with the lay leaders of a church and make them into a cell.

Gradually they warm to it and see its value. It takes them away from an individualistic view of Christianity towards the corporate one which is so dominant in the New Testament. As the Dean of Sabah put it, 'In the past I tried to grow by myself, but when I fell down there was nobody to help me. And when I had problems nobody knew about them. But in a small cell we are responsible for one another. Indeed the first task of the cell is to build that deep quality of relationship with one another that will enable us to move out and reach people who are not yet Christians.' Many of the cathedral members now belong to cell groups, but not all. The transition is neither uniform nor fast.

In Albert Vun's church in Sabah the transition to a cell church structure was far from easy. He worked on it in his teaching and preaching for six years once he became convinced that the Bible study groups of his traditional evangelical church were an inadequate instrument for Christian growth and proved unattractive to new believers. Here again he began by starting with the leaders, putting them in groups, watching them catch fire at the concept, and then teaching about it to the congregation. He feels that the understanding of the Bible has actually grown through this cell structure. It is no longer understood solely in terms of propositional truth but in terms of relationship and application to life. 'We cannot actually live God's word without relationship,' he maintains. And in the cell, relationship becomes second nature.

It must not be thought that there is no variation in cell life in Singapore, or that the Singaporean pattern is normative for the rest of the Province. In parts of West Malaysia the cells are very loose-textured and do not have any particular style: it depends on the location and the membership.

Canon Ng Moon Hing of Ipoh confesses that to begin with he had no idea how cells worked, and he learnt by trial and error. His approach is much more relaxed than that in Singapore or Sabah. The aims are the same: mutual ministry and multiplication. They put a lot of emphasis on the quality of lifestyle, which elicits comments and surprise. People are drawn in by the love and concern of the members. They make much of birthdays and festivals. They are so relaxed in relationships that there is no discernible beginning to the group's activities; they just move into it. They do not have Bibles in the group because it proves a threat to people from other faiths, but members bring verses of Scripture written out on paper, and contribute these. They erect the minimum hurdles. After a while the leader speaks briefly and then, over refreshments, questions and answers flow. When people are out of a job or ill they are prayed for, but this is no shibboleth. It just arises naturally as need dictates. When Moon Hing began cell groups, he called them care groups and invited everyone in each group to bring at least one other person, church member or not, into the group. That is how they began to grow, and now 70 per cent of the church is in cell groups, as the members prefer to call them.

Cell churches are not a cure for all ills. They have weaknesses. In particular they can lead to a low level of biblical knowledge because so much of the teaching depends on the cell leaders who are themselves only lightly trained. They can lead to disunity unless there is strong leadership and the leaders are themselves closely wedded to the vision of the church as a whole. They can be over-controlled from the top, and in a rigid structure they can inhibit the initiative of members. But they are an extremely flexible and effective tool for spreading the gospel. They have made waves in Latin America, among the Pentecostals, the Anglicans and the Roman Catholics. So they have in parts of North America and Europe. They ideally meet the needs in schools and universities. They revolutionize the vitality and outreach of churches.

Cell churches are on the increase in the West. They have become increasingly appropriate in the face of opposition and the marginalization of Christianity. We sometimes forget that the majority of Jesus' ministry was not from the pulpit but in the small cell with twelve members. Perhaps Christians in the West should take more seriously the example of their Lord and his Asian Tigers!

4

Learning about Churchplanting

————◄●►————

All over this region of South East Asia they are seeking to
plant churches. This may be partly due to the pressures of
surrounding society on a comparatively small Christian
minority. But it is largely due to the missionary zeal which is
so marked a feature of all four dioceses in the Province. The
methods are much the same. Start small in a home, often in
a cell. Develop, train and nurture lay leadership. Give them
encouragement, practical resourcing and some finance in the
early days for a limited period. Do not wait for a clergyman
or a building, but allow the lay leadership to found the
church.

There is usually a definite cut-off period which in fact
strengthens the plant because it forces it to take responsibility.
These outposts then become mission churches and in due
course, if they succeed, parishes. The church plant is lay-led
and the clergyman comes round from time to time to conduct
the sacraments. Unlike their Western cousins they do not wait
until they have enough money or resources to start. They do
not put money into bricks and mortar, but into people. If they
need a building larger than a house they hire one. Let us listen
to some of their leaders, in very different places, as they speak
about the churchplanting that they are all attempting.

Canon Ng Moon Hing is the vicar of a large and thriving
Anglican church in Ipoh, West Malaysia. Evangelism is difficult in West Malaysia because the ethnic Malays, who are
passionately Muslim, govern the country, and it is utterly
illegal to evangelize a Malay. It happens, of course, but it is
very dangerous, and the people concerned go underground
and try to leave the country: life is made impossible for them

if they stay. So in practice evangelism takes place among the Chinese and the Indian Malaysians. Moon Hing's church is primarily Chinese. He not only leads an exciting church at St Peter's, Ipoh, where I have had the privilege of ministering more than once, but has had extensive experience of founding churches throughout the diocese over several years. He places the utmost emphasis on lay training. He laid the foundations for this very shrewdly.

Before taking any initiatives in this area he secured the backing of the PCC. The idea was very foreign to most of the church people, who regarded ministry as exclusively the job of their vicar. So he had to woo them by example. In the early days he found that nobody cleared up after church and put the lights out. So he did it himself. Gradually people came to see their responsibility, and the first glimmerings of lay ministry were born. He proceeded to several levels of training. He has training classes in basic Christianity, embracing new believers or people just enquiring about the faith. The class goes on all through the year, and is fed from casual people who just come to try out the church. Wisely, he runs this class himself. But the church also runs membership classes, leadership classes and lay theological classes culminating in a degree. He has realized that the best way to grow is to mobilize the sleeping giant of the laity, and he is doing just that with notable success. So much so that there are now many clergy in West Malaysia who have had their initial training at his hands, and he has seven more in seminary at this time. Before going to seminary they spent time as lay assistants in his church, learning the trade on the job in a lively church – an immense privilege. Only last year one of these men emerged from seminary and was sent to a small struggling church of 60 people, whose numbers had not grown for ten years. In one year the regular attendance has grown to 150. That speaks volumes for the effectiveness of the training which Moon Hing has instilled into them before they ever set foot in seminary. He takes them out to do missions, outreaches in evangelism and village work. They engage in meeting social needs, particularly tutoring poorly educated people. They rent or borrow a house, and the local people are drawn, by curiosity in the first instance, to the vibrant worship which goes on in it. He speaks of one such church founded only eighteen months ago which is now 60 strong and is looking forward to achieving parish status. He and his colleagues have planted no less than 38 Chinese-speaking churches in recent years. Seven of them have failed, but the net gain of 31 is enormous.

These churches may be launched from a few households living in the same area, or a couple of cell groups. They are entirely lay-led. Moon Hing trains the leaders, and they teach and lead the church, while he comes around once a month to celebrate communion.

Moon Hing makes use of cells, like most of the other growing churches in the region. But he is not tied to them. A good deal of the growth is due to the church's caring emphasis: they have a motto 'We care to send and we send to care.' In the course of their caring for local needs they concentrate on special categories of people, including the interested or the lonely, and use festival occasions to invite them to. Twice a year they have harvest dinners, which are well prepared affairs, and culminate in a challenge to begin Christian discipleship.

The Indian churches of West Malaysia are also growing. It was good to discuss the situation with Bishop Moses Poniah, the assistant bishop of West Malaysia. He calls himself a very traditional Anglican, and yet he himself has planted churches. He came to work as Rector of St Christopher's, Johor Baru, which was not interested in mission at all. Gently he began to teach and encourage them to look round. Before long they identified five areas where churches might profitably be planted. He told me:

About four years ago we started visiting in a town about 20 miles away, from which three people came to St Christopher's. Soon we planted a small group in the home of one of these gentlemen, which met on a Friday night. Then they said, 'We must have a service.' So we started service in that house, and it began to grow. Within a year it grew into thirty, forty, fifty and so we had to move to a larger house. St Christopher's Church made all sorts of opposition. They didn't think it was necessary to plant a church because we were still doing building work at St Christopher's. But we kept on pushing and the Lord has blessed us. Today we have bought a double shop lot for this church plant, and St Christopher's has given half the price of it!

All of this has motivated the parent church, St Christopher's. They are prepared to take the lion's share of the financial needs of the plant. What is more, instead of the original single cell round the bishop, they now have 11. And those cells have undertaken the responsibility of planting a church in the other four areas that were identified in the first instance.

The bishop was very interesting on the subject of mobilizing a church for planting new congregations, especially when it is very traditional and frankly opposed to anything of the sort, as his church had been. We have many similar church situations in England. He stresses that the minister must have a burden for mission, that he must regularly teach the congregation about it, and that the whole enterprise from first to last must be soaked in prayer. 'We need to wait on the Lord to show us where to plant.' He is convinced that the Lord will give the direction, draw the people and supply the leadership. Interestingly, the leader in this fruitful plant he was speaking about is a young man who does a secular job for four days a week and works for the church in the other three. He has a real burden for church ministry. The bishop encouraged him to go for theological training. But he has not, hitherto, agreed, maintaining that a theological college would kill him! The bishop is gently seeking to change his mind! Meanwhile, it is instructive to see how Bishop Moses goes about training this man and three or four others. 'Basically the person follows me, watches me, and we have regular training sessions in which we go through various parts of Scripture, carefully choosing passages that are relevant to budding leaders.' At the same time, they will prepare the passage they are going to speak on in the near future, and the bishop will help them with their preparation. This seems to be admirable training, and should not be beyond any parish priest in Britain as a way of developing competent lay leadership.

I found the bishop most refreshing. As he claims, he is a very traditional Anglican, saying the daily offices whether anyone is with him in church or not. In Lent for 36 days he and a number of his people meet early in the morning for worship and teaching. He has Bible teaching sessions both midweek and on Sunday mornings after the eucharist, which they begin at 8.30 – they do not go home until 12.30! He has also inaugurated a monthly service for healing which is drawing increasing numbers, and some of his church members, though fearful, are learning to pray with those who come forward for ministry. And they are seeing clear answers to their prayers. He told me of a boy who had a terrible accident and was thought to be practically dead. The parents were members of the church, and invited the cell group leaders to come to the house and pray. 'We held hands and prayed like mad, and there was a powerful healing – the news spread like wildfire and people realized that the Lord answers prayer.'

It is clear from all this that churchplanting is central to the Christian philosophy of the region, whether they claim evangelical, catholic or charismatic labels. For instance, you find the cathedral at Kota Kinabalu in Sabah hosting no less than ten congregations, on a Sunday. I went into the Filipino congregation, which had only emerged recently. I was interested to discover how. Apparently some Filipina maid-servants had come across the work of the cathedral, and had asked for shelter and support. At the invitation of the diocese, a Filipino mission team came over to get them together in the first instance, and left a worker behind who now looks after a thriving and growing group of forty or fifty. Other congregations started because of a particular need – youth, restaurant workers, young professionals, and healing services. These are quite separate congregations all using the same building – and that is certainly one of the effective ways of churchplanting.

In the industrial city of Sandakan I saw the start of a new Anglican congregation based in a shop. In the interior they are now tending to inaugurate each new church with the definite aim of planting its own church in a few years. Where that has been part of the founding vision, the execution is much easier than in a long-standing traditional church.

But often the churchplanting starts with the recognition of a need among, for example, homeless people or Indonesian immigrants. Those with passion and gifting for evangelism seek to lead one person in this people group to Christ. Then others begin to come along: one, two, three and the number grows. Soon you have a cell and then a congregation. What they do for people groups they also do for localities. Archdeacon Albert Vun told me of a housing estate some distance from him where they have recently planted three churches, each speaking a different language. And it all sprang from a single cell! They call such congregations 'a church without walls' and rate them highly, because they are aware that so often a church building isolates the congregation from the community, while Christians gathering in an ordinary building are much less threatening to the surrounding non-Christians.

It is becoming apparent in some places that it is appropriate to set up special churches for young people. In 1998 I had the privilege of speaking to a crowded stadium in Kuching, Sarawak, on the occasion of their celebrations for 150 years of the Anglican Church in the country. It is characteristic of the enthusiasm of these Sarawak Christians that they determined to give an evangelistic emphasis to this celebration. As it turned out, the response was overwhelming, and some 350 young people swarmed forward to indicate their commitment to Jesus Christ. So when, two years later, I met Edric Ong, who heads up the youth work in the diocese, I asked him how the youth work had developed in the wake of that rally. It seems that the leaders had organized the young people who responded in the stadium into different groups and taken them to the youth centre, called the Shelter, where they were gradually built up. Now some 200 of the English-speaking young people form part of the growing number of youth churches in the diocese, while the Iban-speaking youth are also growing in numbers and commitment. The diocese of Kuching is by far the largest of the four which go to make up this Province, and their youth work is very fruitful. They are planning to reach out in a variety of ways: through a sports outreach, through arts and crafts, and through help with revision for school work. They are planning to hold the first Provincial Youth Missions Congress in Telupid in May. There, in that jungle town in the heart of Sabah, they expect to have some 6,000 young people gathering for a week. They will have three days of concentrated training, followed by three days of practical evangelism in the jungle villages, accompanying some of the local young people from those villages who will also have been at the congress. The long-term aim of this gathering is to mobilize a great company of devoted young Christians to undertake missionary work both at home and in the outlying countries of the South East Asian region. Edric and his task force are clear that the best way to reach young people is through young people themselves. Once their hearts are touched and they have some understanding of the gospel they do not need to be entertained, as we tend to do in Britain, but to be sent out, with an appropriately contextual-ized approach, in mission to their peers.

It seems to me that the Anglican Church in the West could find the Asian experience a helpful spur and example. To be sure, we in Britain have some distinguished churchplanters like Bob and Mary Hopkins and George Lings. Moreover, *Breaking New Ground* was an important Report on churchplanting in the Church of England commissioned by the House of Bishops in 1994. But our record of actually planting new Anglican churches is less than impressive. We need more of the Asian passion, their restless determination to reach out, their confidence in lay leadership, their willingness to start small, their freshness of approach. We are indeed starting to move in this direction despite being hampered by having too many church buildings in Britain, many of which are in the wrong place or in need of expensive repair. There are many areas of Britain however, where we need to plant new churches. For planting is not only a gospel necessity: it is a sign of life.

5

Learning about Leadership

I think the area of leadership is one of the great differences between the Asian Tigers and the Western church. They are very clear about this. Leaders must lead. The Asian church-men teach leadership. They train emerging leaders. They hold leaders accountable.

We do none of these things. Leadership ability seems to be relatively unimportant when men or women are chosen for ordination training in the West. In the ministerial formation itself, there is usually little or no training in leadership, though there is much in biblical criticism and Greek. Nobody is discarded from a theological college because they do not display gifts of leadership. But if they are devoid of leadership qualities, they are likely to be a disaster in a parish. Since they are not confident leaders themselves they either will get pushed around by strong characters in the church and compensate by becoming autocratic, or will resort to a committee decision on everything. Neither of those expedients make for visionary advance. You only have to look at your average PCC meeting to be aware of that. If we get strong leaders in the Western church, it is by accident. And even then there is unlikely to be any accountability. They do their own thing, and most of their parishioners are reasonably content to let them do so, thankful that they belong to a church which is going somewhere.

The ordained leadership of the church

I was very impressed to stay with the bishop of Sabah some time ago and discover his method of training ordinands. First of all he would interview them at length and satisfy himself that they had a lively relationship with Jesus Christ. He knew they would be a disaster in the ministry without that. He then set about assessing whether they had any leadership abilities. He put them in leadership positions under supervision in their own church for a year or two, to see how they did. If they passed this test, they were sent to theological college. After that they were not immediately ordained, but put to work on probation in a congregation under a good parish priest for a further year to see if they had the actual ability to lead a church.

I think of a fascinating afternoon with the bishop of Bunbury in Australia, who is cast in much the same mould. He first of all satisfies himself of the genuine, deeply committed faith of the candidate, and then puts him to work for a couple of years in a run-down church which would otherwise close. If he makes the grade, he does a year or perhaps two in a theological college before ordination. That has transformed the situation in Bunbury Diocese within a few years. In Indonesia, it is not possible to be ordained in some of their fast-growing denominations unless you have started a congregation from scratch and reached the number of thirty or so. To write down these examples seems like stating the obvious. Leaders must lead. It is no good ordaining them if they can't. But in point of fact such examples as I have quoted are very rare and rather shocking in the West. The number of our ordinands would be decimated if they had first to rescue a dying church or form a new congregation. But wouldn't those who passed the test be an impressive leadership cadre?

Well, that is the attitude towards ordination taken by the Asian Tigers. They want leaders who can get things done. They look for leaders who will take risks and show initiative, men whom others will be glad to follow. And they get them. I am enormously impressed by the quality of leadership in most of the clergy I have met in these four dioceses. They do not have the academic qualifications of our ordinands, but they have a passion for souls and a vision of how to lead a parish into renewal and outreach that leaves our people far behind.

Leadership qualities

There is a developing consensus among growing churches that leadership is the single most important factor in growth. The churches of South East Asia are clear that they need pastors who are strong leaders. When you get leaders who are visionary, dynamic, positive and inspirational you generally get growth. That is the situation which applies in Singapore. The Church of Our Saviour is a case in point. It was a church which had long since reached its plateau until it received a new, visionary pastor in Derek Hong, who had the gift of leadership. Then it leaped into spectacular and sustained advance. That is no less obvious in the entirely different situation in the interior of Sabah, where Archdeacon Fred David is at work. He is a born leader and has spearheaded a remarkable work in the jungle, bringing whole villages over to the faith. I was amazed both by the numbers concerned and by the spiritual insight and maturity that they had acquired. It was learned from Fred.

Field Marshal Montgomery once observed, 'Leadership is the capacity and will to rally men and women to a common purpose, and the character which inspires confidence.' Leaders are the thinkers, the inspirers, the motivators, the visionaries. They are those whom people choose to follow. They are the people who make things happen. And that is a God-given charism which should figure very high on our list of qualities for those aspiring to ordination. At present, regrettably, it is not high enough.

In his book *Growing Churches – Singapore Style*, Keith Hinton draws attention to important characteristics of true leadership, which he has seen in the best churches in Singapore, and I agree with him.

Not autocrats

In the first place a leader is not an autocrat. He is aware of having been placed by God in a position of leadership but does not throw his weight about. There is a hierarchy attached to leadership but the true leader does not depend on the hierarchy for his impact. It comes from his Lord. At least, that is the ideal. I do not think the pastors in Singapore entirely manage to avoid the temptation to autocracy, but they would repudiate it in principle. It is significant, I think, that bad leadership in the West tends (on democratic principles) to retreat into the lowest common denominator of committee life. In the East bad leadership operates much more on the model of the Old Testament kings, especially David, and gives way to a somewhat ruthless autocracy. They are equal and opposite temptations.

Not democrats

This leads in to a second most important lesson which the Asian Tigers can teach us. A true leader is not necessarily democratic. Democracy has become the watchword, almost a *sine qua non* in the West, but it derives from the political arrangement of a small Greek city state in the fifth century BC, rather than from anything to be found in Scripture. The good leader will be winsome, gracious and humble. He will consult widely, but when all is said and done the task of a leader is to lead. If you are too far out in front of your people, they will not follow you. If you are too egalitarian, there will be nothing to follow. The difficult art is to be in solidarity with them but one step ahead of them. This step is not arbitrarily taken but derives from the study of Scripture, the needs of the situation, the considered opinion of colleagues, and, most important of all, the visionary charisma of the leader himself. We can get much too excited about the importance of democracy! There is not much danger of any leaders in the West failing to consult widely. There is real danger of their abdicating leadership to keep the committee or the constituents happy.

Those who, like the American church growth expert, Lyle Schaller, have given sustained examination of what makes churches grow, are convinced that a democratic form of church government ends up producing an 'odourless, colourless and tasteless' programme. It is designed to suit everyone but in fact hamstrings the church for further advance. Just think of your PCC. Are you excited by its agenda? Are you thrilled when the night of the PCC meeting comes round? If not, Lyle Schaller and his co-workers may be on to something! Certainly the Asian Tigers have no doubt about the critical importance of a leadership which is neither autocratic nor democratic, but mirrors the servant leadership of Christ and the firm shepherding oversight of God the Father.

Not administrators

These men do not spend a lot of time sitting on committees or in offices. Their leadership is inspirational and up-front. For a leader is oriented towards people, while an administrator is oriented towards tasks. The leader has the vision. The administrator implements it. Of course, some people combine in themselves both administrative and leadership gifts, but if the administrative is allowed to predominate the church will find itself moving towards maintenance rather than growth. On the whole it is good, as the church grows, for the leader to remove himself more and more from the administrative side, in order to remain, as Professor Eddie Gibbs once memorably put it, 'free to roam the growing edge and prepare for tomorrow as much as to preserve yesterday'. We could do with more of that style of leadership in the UK, where the managerial model has been put forward as an ideal in church circles and emulated a lot in recent years. Asia knows well that leaders initiate, while managers manage.

Not enablers

In the West we have seen a lot of emphasis on the servant
ministry as opposed to the man who is six feet above con-
tradiction. There is no doubt that we have the example of
Jesus for this, but in that famous foot-washing occasion we
tend to forget that Jesus told them, 'You call me Master and
Lord, and so I am.' While washing their feet he remained
their authoritative leader, and expects us to follow his
example. The enabler recognizes that different members of
the body of Christ have different gifts, and tries to allow
them space to be expressed. That is a great step forward from
the one-person ministry which so inhibits growth. But it is
inadequate, all the same, and the Chinese have realized it.
Their leaders are not so much enablers as equippers. They
do not merely gain a vision from God of what goals their
church should have, but they train the members so that those
goals are commonly owned and become achievable. There is
a possible weakness in their approach: it almost implies that
the vision is something that will be vouchsafed to the leader
alone or pre-eminently. This is not so. The vision may emerge
from any member of the congregation and can be seen to be
God's leading if it commends itself to the congregation as a
whole. The leader needs to acclaim it and equip for it, but
does not need necessarily to be the visionary himself.

Dynamic leadership

There are many books on leadership these days, and one of
the most helpful is by Leighton Ford, *Jesus, Leader of Men*.
He points out that so much that passes for leadership is transactional, based on rewards in exchange for performance. But
there is another kind of leader, who transforms the situation
he finds – John F. Kennedy and Pope John Paul are two
obvious examples.

- Transactional leaders work within the situation. Transforming leaders change it.

- Transactional leaders accept the agenda of the institution. Transforming leaders change it.
- Transactional leaders accept the rules and values of the organization. Transforming leaders may well change them.
- Transactional leaders talk about payoffs. Transforming leaders talk about goals.

On any showing the greatest transforming leader the world has ever seen is Jesus of Nazareth. One has only to reflect for a moment to see some of the qualities that went to make up that transforming leadership of his.

First, he lived close to God. His life was lived in intimate relationship with his Abba, his dear heavenly Father. He delighted to do the Father's will. He accepted the imperative of obedience 'The Son of man must suffer . . .'

Second, he knew who he was. What he did proceeded out of who he was. And he was very clear about his identity. He knew he was God the Father's only Son, and his whole ministry flowed out from that. What we are is much more important than what we do, and if we are not clear about our identity (as opposed to our status and position in life) we shall always be wondering what people are thinking about us and therefore be quite unable to lead.

Third, Jesus had a clear vision. Karl Marx concluded his Communist Manifesto with the words 'You have a world to win.' That was leadership. Jesus had the vision of founding an alternative society which he called the Kingdom of God, and he subordinated everything to the achieving of that vision. Managers want to do things right, but leaders want to do the right thing, and they have the vision and sheer guts to go for it.

Fourth, Jesus displayed a magnetic example. He completely practised what he preached. That can be demonstrated in detail from the Gospel accounts. We shall never achieve his perfect correspondence between precept and practice, fallen human beings that we are. But unless there is a very substantial correlation between the two we will rightly be branded as hypocrites and our influence will inevitably disappear.

Fifth, Jesus equipped his followers. Not for him the large managerial desk after treading on many people to get to the top. He stood underneath his followers in order to equip them for leadership. That is very evident from the Gospels. Initially he set the example while his followers watched. Then he gave them a small part in the work (like collecting the left-overs after the Feeding of the Multitude). Then he gave them a limited assignment, going out two by two for companionship and mutual stimulus and correction, as in the Mission of the Twelve or of the Seventy. And in due course he stepped back and returned to his Father in heaven, having entrusted the whole enterprise into their care. It was a classic example of training by apprenticing. And look how it paid off in the Acts of the Apostles! They had been spectators of Jesus at work, then apprentices, then partners, then successors. They do that sort of equipping a great deal in South East Asia. We do not do it much in Britain. The results speak for themselves.

Sixth, Jesus lived by an authority derived from Scripture. Not from tradition, or expediency, or the climate of the times, but he built his ministry out of Scripture. 'It is written' was for him the clinching argument, and all his major initiatives, all his self-understanding, all his core teaching sprang from that source. They try very hard to make Scripture their norm in South East Asia. Do we?

Seventh, Jesus embodied love and warmth. There was nothing cold, bookish or distant about him. He was people-centred, and he loved them. I fear that some of our clergy do not really like people: they like books, committees or further degrees. We do not train them with people, but with essays. Yet you have to love people, with all their quirks and failings, if you are to become a transformational leader.

Eighth, Jesus was radical and challenging. Nowhere do you find such a radical analysis of human nature, and such radical action for others. Moreover, he dared to challenge. He challenged the rich, the prostitutes, the demonized, the political and ecclesiastical leaders. This was never done to show off, always to serve the truth. We need leaders who are prepared to stand up like that and be counted. We have some, thank God, but not enough.

Ninth, Jesus was willing to sacrifice. Leadership is costly. It is costly to persevere despite the knocks, to be unjustly attacked without hitting back, to bear pain rather than inflict it, to be totally committed to the welfare of those you serve. Jesus did all that, and endured the cross as well. He offers a model of self-sacrifice which is immensely costly but incredibly attractive. Leaders who, like Churchill and Garibaldi, offer their followers 'blood, tears, toil, sweat' and are prepared to face it themselves – these are the leaders who change the world.

Finally, Jesus was vulnerable. Vulnerable to exhaustion, loneliness, criticism, pain and death. When others see us shed our masks and come over as the frail human beings that we are, albeit fuelled by the grace of God, they will love us deeply and respect us more. Perhaps South East Asia, like Britain, needs to learn afresh that important lesson of leadership.

My observation is that whether consciously or unconsciously the leaders I have met in South East Asia try to make characteristics like these, so superbly exhibited in Jesus, their model. They have not so much modelled themselves on the missionaries or the traditional clergy pattern. While that prevailed, the growth was minimal. But now that they have found themselves under vigorous indigenous leadership they have tended to adopt these crucial characteristics from their Master. I would love to see them more intentionally required in the qualities requisite for ordination in our church.

Theological college students in the West are trained to do the things that churches do, but they are not taught to strategize for growth, or even how to gain a philosophy of ministry. In the Province of South East Asia there is, of course, some blind following of previous traditions, but that is not the prevailing mode. They are imbued with possibility thinking. Much of the failure of the church to grow is due to impossibility thinking, and we have plenty of it in the West. These people with far less resources and experience, in an equally hostile urban environment, seek leaders who expect God to act and are prepared to make great sacrifices in order to see the vision take shape. They will have a very clear goal. Perhaps it is geographical – a block of flats. Perhaps it is linguistic – the Hokkien speakers. Perhaps it is generational – a church for the teenagers. But there is a clear delineation of goals, then a wholehearted commitment to prayer, acts of kindness, penetration of the area, entertainment, witness bearing, conversion and nurture. The Christians believe it before they see it. And God honours faith like that.

Let me give you a few examples. In Sabah the Anglican Church has been led by God to go for a single-minded mission aim, called Harvest 113. It is very simple. They expect each church member of whatever age or background to befriend and win one person into full church membership, within three years. From the bishop downwards this has been the plan. Everybody understands it and owns it. And in the first three years of the programme they are almost up to their goal. They write songs about 113, and church members learn them and act on them! They have conferences on this 'harvest' theme – I spoke at one, and was thrilled by the commitment, vision and wholeheartedness of the participants. The conference sessions last almost throughout the day, as is normal in that part of the world, leaving only three hours in the middle of the day for the sacred siesta, when only mad Englishmen are abroad. I suggested that some of these enthusiastic evangelists might even like to use that time in getting alongside people on the park benches, in the streets or shops or restaurants. I wonder what the response to such a suggestion would have been in the West? But they needed no further invitation! I wish you could have been with me at the five o'clock session when they came back, thrilled and exhausted. It was a marvellous privilege to hear the stories that poured out from them. Many had tried without success, of course, but they had tried. That was the point. Others had seen fruit and were thrilled to bits. I recall that eleven people professed conversion on the first day, and ten on the second. They were all subsequently baptized and confirmed into the church.

Or take another example. In 1998 the Anglican Church in Sarawak celebrated 150 years of life. I was privileged to be a speaker on that occasion. There was some very intentional outreach, which I do not think would have happened at a diocesan celebration in England. First, they had a tremendous gala in the largest covered stadium in the capital city, Kuching, with all manner of celebrations but culminating in an evangelistic address. People had brought their friends: the place held some six thousand, I seem to recall, and there must have been more than ten thousand crammed in. It was led by a gifted layman. A whole bevvy of helpers had been trained to speak to those who came forward to start or renew their allegiance to Jesus Christ, and the four bishops of the Province presided over this counselling team in the four corners of the building. The response was so large, as it happened, and the area so constricted that the rally was less effective than it might have been: we simply could not get near many of the crowd who wanted to make a commitment. Unquestionably, however, many new believers were added to the church. Later, as part of those same celebrations, we must have had five thousand Christians going round the streets at night, each armed with a candle, in the midst of this predominantly Muslim land. That took a lot of courage and was an entirely new initiative in witness. Nothing like it had been done in Kuching before.

Or let me take one of the early examples of 'possibility thinking' leadership from Singapore itself. Canon James Wong is a real leader. While serving as a curate at the cathedral in 1970, he trained a team of young people to engage in door-to-door evangelism. He also realized that the existing churches in those days were not relating to the explosion of high-rise buildings in which the government was rehousing its citizens. So he and his team visited two of these housing developments and found that they would welcome the presence of the church if it brought community social service with it – youth drop-in centres, childcare centres and so forth. When opportunity offered, he started his first house church on the 24th floor of the Buona Vista estate, and a second the year later, and a third the year after that. It took much prayer, hard work, visiting, socializing, to reach these neighbours and draw them into the services of the church in the home.

In due course these house churches outgrew their premises and became extension centres, and now they are becoming parishes. The Church of the Good Shepherd to which James Wong was appointed in 1972 gave birth to the Chapel of the Resurrection, and now they have fifteen congregations, seven of which are extension centres created in response to local needs. Are they satisfied with this advance, involving thousands of people? Not at all. They have just produced a superb and informative magazine, brilliantly illustrated and flowing with faith in God and love towards needy people. It is called 'Rise up and Go Forward'. It is their response to the challenges of the twenty-first century.

I do not mean to give the impression that all is rosy in the leadership offered in these South East Asian churches. There is the danger of competition. There is the danger of growing stale in a small island where the possibility of moving to a new incumbency is strictly limited. Clergy who have been in a church for some time have nowhere to go except overseas or back to secular employment – which is often regarded as a severe loss of face. Some of the leadership may be tinged with anti-intellectualism. Some of it may be over-addicted to slogans – though these are very helpful for the widespread recognition and ownership of policy. The very fact that so many are first-generation Christians brings problems, too: few pastors in Singapore understand the mentality and problems of the second-generation Christian young people who are reaching their twenties. And there may be a tendency for some clergy to equip lay Christians for tasks in the church and in society and delegate them without themselves sharing in them any more. And of course the nettle of women ministers will have to be grasped. It was not up for discussion in Archbishop Moses Tay's episcopate, but it is an issue which will not go away, especially since the church has many cell church leaders who are women, and the Bible is less explicit than is sometimes thought on the matter. No, the Church of the Province is not perfect in its leadership, but it has massive lessons, particularly of faith, courage, clear objectives and intentional equipping, to teach the Anglican Communion in other parts of the world.

Training lay leaders for the Church

The Asian Tigers are strong on training for leadership. I do not mean theological training in which you take a person away from the area of service he was exercising and put him in a seminary. Nor do I mean putting a person in, say, Sunday School teaching and leaving him or her to sink or swim. I mean intentional, practical training for one of the many ministries in the church of God. Their emphasis on training springs, I believe, from two sources. The first was the acute shortage of clergy when indigenous leadership took over from colonial. The second and by far the most important was the biblical conviction that God has given some sphere of ministry to all members of his church and that the most important function of the ordained ministry is to help people discover what their major contribution to the life of the Christian body is, and to equip them for that task. It goes without saying that the massive development of cell churches which characterize this region would have been utterly impossible without well-trained leaders to lead, motivate and look after them.

The church growth experts are clear that activating the laity in ministry is not only a biblical pattern but also a secret of growth. The plain fact is that churches which do not major on lay ministry rarely grow. They tend to stagnate around the 150 mark. That seems to be the maximum that the one-person pastor can effectively look after. Pastor Yonggi Cho, who leads the Full Gospel Church in South Korea, the largest church in the world, is clear that much of his church's extraordinary growth is due to the effectiveness of the lay ministers who look after home cells of a dozen or so. He is equally clear that many of these are women, that vast untapped source of Christian leadership in many churches. And it is the task of the clergy to train such people. A clergyman like Archdeacon Albert Vun in Sabah spends almost all his time in training and monitoring the vast force of lay pastors who head up the 315 cell churches which comprise his church. It is much the same with Canon Derek Hong in the Church of Our Saviour in Singapore, where they expect to have 600 cells by the year 2001.

Derek's plan of campaign is this. His church operates through cells, who handle the pastoral care and almost every aspect of ministry. The cell is the basic Christian community. His vision is to build a great network of Christ-centred, Spirit-filled communities relating to human needs throughout Singapore and beyond in a way that God can bless. He hopes to establish a home cell in every street in Singapore, to multiply cells from their already large stock, and to make increasing contact with the neighbourhood, using the strategies mentioned previously in the project 'Love Singapore'.

We have seen a good deal about the basic cell structure in a previous chapter. But he develops this much further. Cells in several adjacent estates come together from time to time to form a cluster. There are four cells to a cluster. These cells come in three shapes. One is geographical: they emerge from a common location. A second is professional: the members perform a common function – perhaps as foreign workers, business people or homemakers. A third is composed of people who have common needs or interests – young people, dance and drama groups, tennis players, support groups for various medical conditions and so forth.

The cells meet once a week for half an hour longer than those in Sabah described in Chapter 3. They carry out a cell group programme prescribed centrally, so as to maintain the unified vision of the church. Each cell is expected to grow and multiply within eighteen months. When a cell grows to a dozen or so it splits, and the leader continues with one group while his assistant takes over the other. New cell groups can be started at any time, after consultation with the area pastor. Obviously new cells require a lot of careful supervision and nourishment in the early stages.

The cell leader encourages cell members to attend the equipping classes which are a regular part of the church life. It is well understood that no one denomination is going to have the ability to reach the whole of Singapore, and so cells in housing estates are encouraged to network with other churches in the community. There is not just a passive recognition of each other's denominations, but an active working together for the cause of the Kingdom of God. There is a good deal of dying-to-live in all this. The geo-networks, described in Chapter 2, are growing all over Singapore. And in this geo-network one church will become the key player, the anchor or host church for large-scale network events. I hope and pray that mainstream Western churches will intensify their determination to work in partnership with other denominations. There are encouraging signs that this is happening, and certainly few actions could have greater impact. The illusion that Anglicans are the church of Britain and have pastoral responsibility for all who live within the parish boundaries is utterly unrealistic today, however much it may have applied in the days when Catholics and Non-Conformists were banished! It would make a big impact in ecumenical relations in Britain if the Anglicans did not unconsciously assume a superiority which is often more illusory than real – and very much annoys other denominations! The plain truth is that we need each other, and that often other denominations have a good deal to teach us. Think of the remarkable growth of the Vineyard Fellowships in just a few years. Ten years ago there were hardly any: now most towns have one. Arguably such people have more to teach us than we have to teach them. In a Millennial Statement Roger Forster has drawn attention to the breakdown of denominational barriers in recent years and is confident that this will be the pattern for the next generation. Certainly young people today have little interest in denominations. They go where the life is, and Anglican youngsters are most unwilling to unchurch Methodists, Catholics or Baptist churches in the vicinity. There is no reason in principle (though much in prejudice) to prevent us from adopting the geo-network plan so effective in Singapore.

Needless to say there is in their cell structure a hierarchy of oversight culminating in regular meetings with the vicar. It is critically important to exercise great care over this oversight, or the cells could easily become loose canons doing their own thing, and spawning problems beyond the competence of cell pastors to resolve.

One of the largest churches in the South East Asian Province is, I think, that of Albert Vun in Tawau. As we have seen, it is a cell-based church, and Albert had a number of helpful suggestions about training cell leaders.

In the first place, he regards the vision as determinative. New cell leaders must understand the vision. New wine must be poured into new wineskins, and this whole principle of small groups looked after by lay leadership and mobilized for ministry and mission is a long way from the traditional understanding of the role of the congregation! The new cell leader is called to a daunting role, to a leadership which 'sees more than others see, sees further than others see, and sees before others see'. Albert is convinced that without vision nothing will happen. The new leader must receive the vision from God and carry it out. That was the Pauline pattern: 'Go, for he is a chosen vessel to me to carry my name before the Gentiles, and kings and the sons of Israel; for I will show him how great things he must suffer for my name's sake.' Paul was not disobedient to the heavenly vision, and neither must cell leaders be. They must commit their lives to looking after those in his cell, equipping them for Christian witness and service, and then splitting half of them off under other leadership so that the whole may increase.

Second, a cell leader needs to take up the leadership. Albert is rightly convinced that if you are going to change the direction of an organization you need to change the leader. It was so in Joshua's day (Joshua 1.9–11) and so it is still. He is concerned to build up a strong network of significant people, rock solid on the foundation of their call and gifting on the one hand and the crucial importance of the cell to the body on the other. With those convictions they must set out to lead.

His third priority is to build up strong Sunday services. It is a great mistake to imagine that if you have multiple cells you need not bother about the Sunday celebrations. I find it fascinating that Albert, who has built the largest network of cells in the province, has also built a vast church building for his people to come together and celebrate on a Sunday. We need the small group for nurture and encouragement. We need the large celebration for stimulus and the sense of belonging to a great movement, the church catholic throughout the world. The Sunday services there are two hours in duration, and every minute counts. Preaching is crucial. He listens to his own tapes several times over in order to improve. But the supreme aim of the Sunday service is twofold: to deepen the intimacy with God of every worshipper and to deepen their faith that 'God is able to do exceedingly abundantly above all that we ask or think'. They have an hour's prayer meeting beforehand – a bit different from a formal prayer with the choir! And he seeks in every service to further the spiritual direction of the church. He looks for spiritual authority, coming from the Word of God, and spiritual momentum, coming from the responsive action of the people. In a word, he is out to raise the faith atmosphere in the congregation, remembering that Jesus could do little in his own home town because of their unbelief (Mark 6.5, 6). Without faith there is no spiritual power. And if Anglicans do not express that faith, God will sadly have to dispense with them and work through those who do in fact trust him and risk for him. Albert Vun is out to reduplicate the Joshua and Caleb generation, who trusted God against the odds. True faith comes from hearing the word of God, agreeing with it, and going out to obey it.

The training up of strong, persistent intercessors is a vital principle for all spiritual advance. While all Christians are called to pray, God gives to some Christians a particular ministry in intercession like the Lydia fellowship in Britain. Often they are older members of the congregation who have had a lot of spiritual experience but are incapacitated by age and bad health from doing much active work. They can become a powerful corps of intercessors, and need to be properly informed of what is going on, what is needed, and the hopes and aspirations of the church leadership. Albert loves that verse in Isaiah, 'I have posted watchmen on your walls, O Jerusalem; they will never be silent day or night. You who call on the Lord, give yourselves no rest and give him no rest until he establishes Jerusalem and makes her the praise of the earth' (Isaiah 62.6, 7). The establishing of a core group of persistent praying people is one of the fundamentals of renewal.

Albert's next principle of leadership training is to hire and train a strong staff team. They need not be ordained – that is one of the mistakes which some parts of the Anglican Communion have made. But they do need to exhibit gifts which can be trained for significant ministry in some aspect of the church's life. Training and lifestyle are to mark the leadership at all levels. You cannot expect the church to move if the leaders are stationary. When the children of Israel crossed the Jordan into the Promised Land, it was the priests who went first and stepped into the water (Joshua 3.14–17). That is still God's way.

There is another aspect of quality leadership – the ability to focus on the crucial issue. Sometimes when God calls us to take a new direction we need to have the courage and single-mindedness to forsake the old in order to embrace the new. The church needs to focus on what is essential, and it will be the leadership which keeps calling the church to do just this. I recall Albert Vun, in an address to international leaders, drawing attention to Nehemiah 6.1–4, where Sanballat, Tobiah and Geshem invited Nehemiah to extended discussions. And Nehemiah, consumed with the desire to get the walls of Jerusalem built, replied 'I am carrying out a great work, and I cannot go down. Why should the work stop while I go down to you?' Four times the invitation was issued, and four times the same answer was given. Discourteous? Perhaps. But very clearly focused. We could do with a bit more of that focus in the West. They have it in Asia.

Finally, Albert Vun is anxious to inculcate in his cell leaders the principle of sacrifice, which of course runs at the very heart of authentic Christianity. He wants men and women who are prepared for the long haul, and prepared to pay the price. 'Sacrifice', he observes, 'is the measure of ownership of the vision. The higher the level of leadership people want to reach, the greater the sacrifices they will have to make.'

As I observe the state of the Anglican Communion in the West, after considerable exposure to it, it seems to me that our cousins in South East Asia, albeit one of the smallest and newest Provinces of our Communion, have hit on some fundamental principles that we need to embody if, like them, we are to experience explosive growth. There is no growth without sacrifice.

6

Learning about God's Powerful Spirit

———◆———

Spirituality is a subject we reckon to know something about in Western church circles. Often we broaden our conception of the word and include various types of Eastern spirituality, including transcendental meditation and Zen Buddhism. We affirm shamanism, and American Indian and Maori worship, and we appreciate the ecologically correct attitudes of a revived paganism. Broader still, the New Age, with its channellers and crystals, its pseudo-science and its health foods, joins the mélange of spiritual potions in many an Anglican's world view. We are very broad-minded when we talk about spirituality. We know about these things.

So it is a shock to go out to South East Asia and find that the Anglican Christians will have nothing to do with any of these other spiritualities. Most of them are first-generation believers, so fast is the gospel growing in their part of the world. They have been Buddhists, Confucianists, Taoists or animists, and they have left it all behind. They now refuse to have anything to do with any worship or world view that has the sniff of idolatry about it. Most of them have, in the past, been captive to these forms of spirituality, and they have found them oppressive. To break with them has been difficult and socially costly, but you do not find them wanting to go back. They know, as St Paul knew, that whereas the names given to the pagan gods may be unimportant, the spiritual forces unleashed on those who worship idols is very real. Thus St Paul can say without inconsistency, 'We know that an idol is nothing at all in the world and that there is no God but one' (1 Corinthians 8.4) and 'The sacrifices of pagans are offered to demons, not to God, and I do not want you to participate with demons. You cannot drink the cup of the Lord and the cup of demons; you cannot have part in both the Lord's table and the table of demons' (1 Corinthians 10.20f.). In the West we are dominated by the concept of cultural relativism and we are very unconcerned if a church member comes to the eucharist and also engages in astrology, freemasonry, Hindu meditation or even a touch of shamanism. To be sure, some churches would frown on these things, but many would be benignly indifferent.

Not so our South East Asian brothers and sisters. They know three things about idolatry in all its forms. First, it has not led them to the true God, but has kept them in ignorance of his love and in fear of unseen spiritual forces. Second, they know the power idolatry used to have over their lives: it is immensely difficult to escape from. Third, it is the sworn foe of the Christian faith. So once set free, you rarely see them experimenting with it again. They believe Western liberal attitudes are not only gravely mistaken but spiritually blind to the power which idolatry exercises in those countries where it holds unhindered sway. Idolatrous practices allow access to spiritual forces which do not derive from God, and which can be very destructive in human lives. Like the Christians of the New Testament and early centuries they praise God for delivering them from the many spiritual tyrants which held sway over their lives. This sense of liberation is the cause of great celebration, and Justin, Athenagoras, Origen, Tertullian and Augustine, to mention but a few of the early Christian fathers, are eloquent about the reality of demonic influence on human lives and the power of Jesus Christ to set men free. The South East Asian Christians have ample precedent for their convictions!

This may all seem rather extreme. But let us look at it from the other end. If they reject the broad expanse of spirituality which Western Christians tend to favour or at least tolerate, what do they have to put in its place?

The answer is quite simply the Holy Spirit. They live with a profound awareness of the powerful Holy Spirit of the living God, and they seek to draw him into everything they do. Life is lived in intimacy with the living, powerful God of whom the Bible speaks. They consciously seek to keep in step with the Spirit. I could illustrate this in a variety of ways. I could give an orderly account of spiritual gifts such as prophecy, healing, tongues, visions, deliverance ministry. But I prefer to introduce you to some of the Christians working in the Province, so that you can enter, so to speak, into the spiritual atmosphere in which they live. This will, I believe, be less contrived and more effective.

Consider, first of all, some of these extracts from the bishop of Sabah's 1999 Christmas letter to his friends. Here is how he begins:

> 'God so loved the world that he gave his one and only Son that whoever believes in him should not perish but have eternal life' (John 3.16). This is one of the first verses that we learned from the Bible. It still has a great impact on our lives – in fact with increasing measure as the years go by. May we in this very last letter of the century share with you these wonderful promises of God for you. May our Almighty God bless you and your loved ones today and into the next century. May Jesus who gave his life for you be your wonderful Saviour. May you experience his comforting and loving presence with you now and always.

The spirituality of this Christian leader leaps from the page: this is just a Christmas letter to his friends! Do you not sense the love and warmth inspired by the Spirit of God?

He continues,

> One of the highlights of the year is that we had the first inter-church pastors and church leaders 'Prayer Summit' in Sabah. In July about 90 church leaders from different denominations came together for three days and two nights to pray and repent before God and to one another of our lack of unity and Godly love. It was a wonderful

time of healing and reconciliation . . . We are now planning another 'Prayer Summit' next year which we hope will be followed by an inter-church open evangelistic meeting. We are all very excited about this.

Or how about the bishop's passion for outreach?

We sent three mission teams out this year, to Perth, Mauritius and Sydney. Our people were greatly encouraged by these mission trips . . . We also sent out our first long term missionary this year. The Rev. and Mrs Chai Lip Vui and their baby left Sabah for Kampuchea in mid-September. They will work among the Chinese speaking Kampucheans. They have a great desire to learn the Kampu-chean language so as to minister to the Kampuchean locals . . . This year we launched WESCAM (West Coast Anglican Mission), a mission initiative of lay people with the clear vision of starting new churches and strengthening the existing worship centres for evangelism and church planting. It is our prayer that there will be a worshipping congregation in every town and district of the West coast of Sabah. Similar plans are being set up for the East Coast and the interior of Sabah . . . Pray that we will not miss any opportunities to share his love with others and that we will move in accordance with his Holy Spirit.

Do you sense that missionary passion inflaming the hearts of bishops in the West? Sometimes, but it is not a notable characteristic yet, I fear.

One of the most anti-Christian of all the Muslim oil states is Brunei, but the bishop writes: 'Under a very tight religious control, it is not an easy place for us to get into, but we thank God that the Anglican churches there are growing.' I know Brunei a bit, and I know how tough things are. To survive is difficult, to grow is wonderful. But that is the passion these believing Christians have, bishop and people alike. They habitually live close to the Lord.

What do you think as you approach your Diocesan Synod? I wonder if the preparation is anything like that in

Sabah? 'Our preparation for the Synod included one month of prayer count-down by the whole Diocese and the intercessors prayed on site throughout the time of the Synod.' And was their agenda typical ecclesiastical discussion? Not at all. They decided to 'reform and revamp' the diocese by dissolving both the Sabah Interior Mission and the Sabah Urban Mission and making all the congregations into new parishes 'for mission and growth'.

It is this awareness of the Spirit of God, this constant attitude of prayer, dependence and obedience, that is so striking for a visitor. Here are the musings of a woman who longs for children but is barren.

> Lord, how I often bewail my physical inadequacy as a woman. How I long to be called Mummy. I know that you would understand. Although biblically you are never addressed as mother, yet you are often portrayed as one with motherly tenderness. You have gently assured me that I am specially made by you – knitted and woven by your perfect hand according to your perfect image under your watchful eyes, and there is no mistake about me. Praise you Lord, for the assurance that I am as complete as any other... Thank you Lord for showing me my identity in you. You hold the key to the locked door. Then let me not try to prise it open but instead seek another door and enter through it. As I moved towards the open door you unfolded your eternal plans for me – a child-free life. I began to discover what I was set free to become and to be involved in – a child blessing ministry. 'Sing O barren woman, you who never bore a child... because more are the children of the desolate woman than of her who has a husband.' Hallelujah! Thank you Lord that I am not childless but child-free, set free to serve! Glory to God.

One of the very moving examples of a woman filled with the Spirit of God is Mrs Cynthia Tay, unmarried at the time of this excerpt but now wife of the bishop. In her devotional time one morning she found her soul flooded with this song, made up of verses from Scripture:

> For thou art great and doest wondrous things.
> Thou art God alone.
> Teach me thy ways, O Lord. I will walk in thy truth.
> Unite my heart to fear thy name.
> I will praise thee O Lord my God with all my heart,
> And I will glorify thy name for evermore.

She knew she was meant to give these verses to someone, and went to the cathedral for morning service – only to find the bishop leading it with those very words! Screwing up her courage this young woman, not even yet a licensed parish worker, thrust them into the hands of the bishop who found, to his amazement and hers, that they spoke very much to his situation. Cynthia had surrendered the whole question of marriage to God some time earlier. She knew that, whether married or single, disenchantment or a chip on the shoulder drives the joy of the Lord from your heart. So she was happy enough as a single woman but joyfully accepted the change, and married Moses, who had been widowed with two teenage children a few years earlier. Then Cynthia recalled a prophecy from a visiting pastor some years earlier that she would marry a man with children! As if this was not enough, a prayer partner, quite ignorant of forthcoming events, passed her a verse of Scripture: 'He settles the barren woman in her home as a happy mother of children. Praise the Lord' (Psalm 113.9).

All of this may seem over the top to Western ears. All too spookily spiritual for us? But listen to the sequel. She and Moses conceived just one child. It was a little girl, dearly longed for. And she was born dead. There appeared to be no medical reason. Imagine the anguish, the sense of betrayal, the complaints before her God. She writes of this most eloquently and movingly in the book *Not Alone*, a superb collection of testimonies about the reality of the living God in a tough unheeding world.

In her grief Cynthia was cast back on the Lord, drew great comfort from him, and was a channel of his love to many who came to comfort her. She recalls how she knew that she needed to go deeper with God, and tells how one particular sympathy card with purple tinted clouds was such a help to her. To her amazement she had had a vision of precisely that picture six months earlier. So 'in awe and wonder I read the Bible verse in the card: "And we know that in all things God works for good for those who love him, who have been called according to his purpose" (Romans 8.28). Can I not trust him for what I cannot understand?' she asked herself. Those who know Cynthia Tay will know what a wonderful woman of God she has become through taking this time of suffering in such a positive way. She is a superb teacher, a wise counsellor, a gracious hostess and above all a deep woman of prayer. I mention this story simply to underline that those who have been filled with the Holy Spirit are in no way shielded from the hardships of life: but they are given a superhuman power to cope with them.

Wherever you go in these dioceses you find people speaking about being baptized with the Holy Spirit. The nomenclature is not helpful, because there are only seven New Testament references to being baptized in or with the Holy Spirit, and they all refer to an initial encounter with the life-giving Spirit of God, not to some second experience. But although the language is not helpful it is very common worldwide, and it points to a time of deep renewing by the Spirit of God which moves Christians into a different gear. It is certainly no mere emotional experience for those with weak minds. Listen to the Very Revd John Tay, Dean of St Andrew's Cathedral in Singapore: 'A significant event in 1976 was my baptism in the Holy Spirit, which brought the gifts of spiritual discernment and other spiritual gifts of the Spirit into my life. The baptism did not come easily to me because I had a long struggle with intellectual blocks.'

At that time he was an academic in the National University of Singapore. He was shown that his life would sustain a threefold reduction or emptying, and sure enough it happened. The bishop replaced him in the church where he was currently a non-stipendiary minister. The family left the nest. And he felt impelled to resign from the university so as to work full-time in the ordained ministry. Not only is he now the dean but he has been active in planting churches in seven provinces of the Philippines and most recently in the cities and villages of Northern Thailand, where the new churches are accompanied by community care projects. That is the practical outcome of his moving into deeper water with God's Holy Spirit.

Canon James Wong is one of the outstanding Christian leaders in Singapore. Launched from tiny beginnings, the Chapel of the Resurrection which he leads now has eight congregations, and runs seven extension centres. His father was massacred by the Japanese and his mother was an illiterate pagan. In due course, through education in Australia, he committed his life to Christ and to full-time service at one and the same time. He pursued his call in a typically Anglican way. As an able young man he went to theological college, was made a deacon in the cathedral, and proceeded to further studies overseas. He was then appointed as the first Asian pastor to the English congregation of the Church of the Good Shepherd – a daunting prospect, and it led him to cast himself on God. He writes,

> I was desperate for God to reveal himself to me in a fresh way. I cried out to him, saying that if he had something new for me I would be ready to receive it. One night as I prayed, I sensed that God was going to do something to answer the longing of my heart. After praying for a while, I became still for a moment. Then I felt my tongue begin to move, and found myself speaking in an unknown tongue. I had no contact with Pentecostal Christians and speaking in tongues was entirely new for me. I concluded that it was God who had given me this new experience and that Jesus Christ had baptized me with the Holy Spirit. I

did not seek the gift of tongues, but God was gracious in giving me this faith-building experience.

He goes on to tell how he discovered that Bishop Chiu had had very much the same experience, as recorded in Chapter 1. And this drew together two men who would not have been natural friends but who became close allies in the renewal which began to sweep over Singapore in the 1970s. The gift of tongues sometimes accompanies this deep entry into the realm of the Holy Spirit, but by no means always. Often the Christian becomes much more susceptible to the guidance of God through dreams and visions. James Wong offers a good example of this. He writes of a 'picture' he had.

> A large ship was in dry dock being repaired and repainted. Soon the water began to rise within the dock and the lock needed to be opened so that the ship could sail out to sea. I concluded that the renewal of the church was like the water rising to a higher level and the time would come for the church to be launched out into the ocean – to active mission and evangelism beyond its present confines.

And now, a quarter of a century later, that vision has come wonderfully true, and the Singapore Anglicans have become one of the great sending agencies in Christian mission.

Sometimes the breaking in of God's Holy Spirit is more drastic. The Rev. Vincent Hoon came from a typical Taoist family, that prayed only on the first and fifteenth day of the month. He was dissatisfied with deities that neither spoke nor answered his requests. In due course he was invited by a friend to a Christian meeting. Some time later there was an evangelistic campaign and he heard the altar call but felt it was unnecessary for him since he had already started going to church. Imagine his surprise when the speaker issued another call for those who thought they were Christians but were unsure of it. This led to his salvation. Later he was challenged to allow the Holy Spirit to come and fill his life. This seemed too costly, and he went out to a coffee shop to think about it. A friend came by and encouraged him to trust God whose plans for him were only good. So he went back for ministry, and found that only the pastor was left. He asked for prayer and was 'slain', that is, rendered unconscious, under the power of the Spirit. He lay there for about an hour. The outcome surprised him. No cosy blessings, but further challenge. He had applied for a place in a Bible college in New Zealand and had twice been refused. But on the third application he was accepted for a degree course, and greatly profited from his studies. However, in his last term he found that he had no money to complete paying his fees. He had given away his last $50 note to help support fellow students going on summer mission trips. Left only with loose change to survive his final weeks at college, he was amazed when, at a small group meeting to which he belonged, a widow handed him an envelope with $50 in it.

> It was like the stories I read in missionary biographies. I was overwhelmed with thanksgiving, and knew that the money for the fees would be forthcoming. The following week, I received an envelope with my name on it. Inside was a New Zealand Post Office cheque for $700, the exact amount for my school fees for the term. I went down on my knees and gave praise to God. He is indeed Jehovah Jireh, our Provider.

Sometimes this deep meeting with God's Holy Spirit leads to gifts of healing.

That was the case with John Savarimuthu, the Indian bishop of West Malaysia. It would be fair to say that in the early part of his episcopate he was rather opinionated and difficult to get on with. I only got to know him after all this had begun to change. His heart was in deep trouble and his consultant told him he must have a triple bypass. He said he was too busy. In due course the operation was rearranged, by which time his condition was very acute. The night before it was to take place Bishop John placed his whole condition before God in prayer, felt a great heat in his chest and fell asleep. When he woke up he was completely healed, and this was confirmed by his consultant. In the few remaining years of his life he had a simply amazing ministry of healing. God used him in an extraordinary way. One of the most remarkable occasions was when he personally petitioned the Prime Minister to allow him to conduct a Christian healing mission in the stadium in the heart of Kuala Lumpur. Can you imagine such a thing in so aggressively Muslim a state as West Malaysia? The results were phenomenal.

When he prayed for people they normally fell to the ground. I remember his coming to a church where I worshipped in Chilwell, just outside Nottingham, at my invitation. Some seventy people gathered to hear the bishop tell what God had done in his life, and then he offered to pray for people. Most came forward and all but a couple fell to the carpet. Many afterwards testified to some area of healing in their lives, and others to a great sense of the love of God for them.

This falling to the ground seems very strange to most of us in the West. I was amazed when I began ministering in South East Asia and found people sinking to the ground as I prayed for them. This did not happen as a result of any particular action or through any agency or technique. Nobody touched them or suggested they should lie on the floor! I think the spiritual atmosphere was so warm that God was able to act in this way. It would be a great mistake to suppose that this sort of thing is just an extravagance of the so-called Toronto Blessing. It happens in many parts of the world, including Britain, and certainly not only among evangelicals and charismatics. I have seen it in Roman Catholic circles. It seems to be a way in which God encourages his children to relax in his love and rest in his faithfulness. I have never known anyone unaffected by the experience when they got up. Some found their mouths filled with laughter, some shed tears of repentance and renewal, some experienced some area of healing, some sensed a fresh direction for their lives and ministries, and some were simply refreshed with a new touch of the love of God. At the conclusion of a major Anglican

Conference for Christian Leaders in Singapore in November 1999, twelve of us who had been speaking were invited to stand at the front at the end of the eucharist and anoint with oil any who so wished for a renewal of their dedication and equipping for their work. Nearly all the 700 or so present came forward, and we all had our hands full for a couple of hours. I asked each person what they wanted to pray for, we prayed, and when I looked up in most instances I found that he or she had sunk to the ground. Was this an emotional trip? I think not. Several saw a call opening before them to serve God in places as tough as Afghanistan and Kashmir. I recall with warm approval a comment of the present archbishop of York on this topic: 'I don't mind people falling down, but I want to know if they are any good when they get up.' These people are!

It is important to recognize how tough and ungullible these Christians are. I think of the Rev. Paul Tan, born among six children in his Buddhist home. When he was converted through a friend's testimony, his father rejected him. One night a visitor from Nagaland, a part of India where there is a major movement towards Christ, prophesied over him that he would be ordained. Not long afterwards he got married, and his sister was set free from demon possession. He and his wife proceeded to follow the call. It meant selling their house in order to get through college, and even then they had nowhere to go before ordination. They learnt to trust God in hard times, and it has proved invaluable in their subsequent ministry.

Another striking example is the Rev. Madavan Nambiar, who grew up in Penang in a Hindu family. Addicted to heroin, he was unable to hang on to any job. First he was hospitalized, then he was locked up in a mental institution for treatment. After coming out he resumed his habit. His father took him to see an Indian priest-medium hoping that through the intervention of the goddess Kali he would be able to change. He had to drink the blood of a chicken and a pigeon, mixed with ashes, and was assured that Kali had removed the desire for drugs. No such luck! He went back to his addiction, slept on the streets in a cardboard box, and in due course was noticed and cared for by a Christian. A pastor took him, filthy as he was, back to his parsonage and spent the whole night in prayer for him. When Madavan awoke he entrusted his life to Christ and found immediately that the craving for drugs had gone. That man is now in the ordained ministry!

One friend of mine, Soh Chye Ann, is another example of living in the power of the Holy Spirit. Born into a family which practised traditional Chinese religion, he became increasingly dissatisfied with it and in due course became a follower of Jesus Christ, thereby drawing down on himself a great deal of odium from the rest of the family. They felt he had betrayed the family and angered the ancestors. Things did not become easier as he set out on the path for ordination! Shortly afterwards, however, his sister was sick to death. Repeated visits to hospitals and temples achieved nothing. She was dying. The family did the sensible thing and asked Chye Ann, 'Can your church help us?' Intense prayer was offered by the Christians, and a miraculous, complete and instantaneous healing took place, while the whole family was gathered around her bed! It is not surprising to hear that they all forthwith became Christians. He and his wife Helen have been missionaries sent out by the Anglican Church in Singapore to South Africa, where they have had a great impact. Chye Ann found himself in a situation where, as a foreigner from outside the racial tensions of South Africa, he had many opportunities to help bring people together in peace and harmony through the gospel. 'That culminated', he writes, 'in a massive Jesus Peace Rally held in the city of Durban in April 1994, days before the crucial National Elections. Thirty thousand Christians gathered to pray for peace and impacted the process which even the secular press hailed as "The day God Saved South Africa".' He is currently the Asia Director of the Church Mission Society, based in London.

One could give many more such examples. But let one suffice, that of the archbishop, Moses Tay himself. He was the fifth child of a Christian school principal, born just before the dark days of the Japanese occupation. There was an unusual sense of expectancy because his mother had received this prophecy before the birth: 'He shall be called Moses. For like the Moses of the Bible who led the Israelites out of Egypt, he shall lead the whole family to leave the secular work in the world for the work of the Lord.' On one occasion when he was a young doctor in his twenties, he felt impelled by God to go to the patient in Bed 3 Ward D1 and share the gospel with him. Naturally he struggled against such an outrageous idea, but the Holy Spirit insisted. He was reminded of the passage in Ezekiel: 'If I say to the wicked "You shall surely die" and you give him no warning nor speak to warn the wicked from his wicked way, in order to save his life, the wicked man shall die in his iniquity, but his blood I will require at your hand.' So he went, found the man receptive and led him to Christ. The next day on ward round he noticed how bright and happy the man seemed. On the third day his bed was empty. He enquired where the man was, and was told he had died. 'The reality of life and death hit me like a thunderbolt – eternal life and eternal death. The event shaped my subsequent course of life. An immediate effect seemed to be a spiritual breakthrough for me. People started inviting me to speak to Christian groups that sought to reach out to non-Christians.' This led in due course to his ordination as a non-stipendiary minister, while continuing to superintend the hospital in Singapore. At that time the wind of the Spirit was sweeping through the island, and he found himself studying Scripture carefully to examine these strange phenomena of tongues, prophetic utterances and falling under the power of the Spirit. It led to a profound experience of the Spirit which has dominated his life ever since. When he was elected, to his great surprise, as bishop, his wife died of a cerebral haemorrhage just two months before his consecration. Being filled with the Spirit is no insurance against hard times. But one morning he was awakened by God, who seemed to say to him just one word, 'Ask'. So he did. He asked for his family and he asked for revival. Both have been wonderfully answered.

Such is the quality of spiritual life in much of the Province of South East Asia. Of course it is not to be found everywhere. Of course there are terrible failures. But it is the prevailing wind, irrespective of churchmanship, nationality, background or culture. And it faces us in the West with a serious challenge. Why is our Christianity so much less intensely aware of God, so much less dynamic than theirs? Why do we not expect to grow, as they do? As we saw in Chapter 1, the multi-faith, pluralist, postmodern urban culture is reasonably similar in both countries. Why are things so different with us?

It would be jejune to jump to any premature conclusions. For one thing the East Asian mindset is a non-restrictive one. People do not put a limitation on things but are always trying to remove restrictions. That is deep in the Taoist culture from which many of them come. As a result the Christians tend to see God in every aspect of their lives. They do not limit him and tell him what he is not supposed to do! They expect the unexpected.

Moreover, it is important to recall that God is sovereign, and there have always been times and seasons throughout history where he has been more active in one part of the world than another. It may simply not be his time for overflowing blessing in the West. Nobody can force God's hand. But we must not be complacent. We would not go far wrong if we concluded that the Enlightenment had had a great deal to do with attitudes in the West. Although it is now in decline, Enlightenment thought with its tendency to reject God, to discredit the miraculous, to exalt human reason and to question everything has for two centuries eaten deep into every corner of the Western world. We are very uneasy with any spectacular and supernatural works of the Holy Spirit and even more uneasy with the idea of influence by demonic powers. We are largely blind to the spiritual battle of which our Asian brothers and sisters are only too well aware.

Moreover, we may well be theists intellectually, but for all practical purposes we are materialists. We are not accustomed to bringing God into every aspect of daily life. We do not expect him to intervene. We do not look his way very often during the day. To be honest, we operate most of the time as if he did not exist. This holds good even for departments of theology in universities and seminaries. We are deeply trapped in the secularist assumptions of our society. I have just come across a remarkable article by an academic in the School of Law in Alabama University. Here is a piece of it.

> The more this country struggles to free itself from religion, the more we become entangled in the consequences. If people are taught that they came from slime, the obvious questions and consequences must follow: What is the purpose of my existence? Hopelessness. Who made you boss over me? Lawlessness. Why are your rules good and mine bad? Relativism. What does it matter how I live if I came from slime and return to slime? Immorality and inhumanity.

We have been seduced by our environment. The Christian mind has largely disappeared. We do not often make serious attempts to think biblically about the issues of the day. We Western Christians are drowning in a sea of relativism, pluralism and scepticism.

It seems to me that we have a simple choice. Either we continue as we are, with the churchgoing statistics plummeting, and the Christian influence in the West diminishing, or else we take a leaf out of the book of these vibrant Asian Tigers. To be sure, they have not got it all right, but they have got a lot more right than we have.

They are right, if politically incorrect, to take an unequivocal stand on the incompatibility of any form of idolatry with Christian commitment.

They are right to lay such emphasis on the need for personal conversion and a serious acceptance of the Bible as the norm for faith and practice.

They are right to make repentance such an important part of their lives, confessing and forsaking sins rather than hiding them, glossing over them or explaining them away.

They are right to open themselves up to the powerful invasion of the Holy Spirit, expecting him to be active in their lives.

They are right to expect not only the graces but the gifts of the Spirit to be manifested among them – healing, prophetic utterance, dreams and visions, the ministry of deliverance and tongues.

These spiritual gifts are far too important to be left to the card-carrying charismatics. They are part of God's heritage for the whole church.

The charismatic movement has been active in Western churches for nearly forty years. We have patronized it, domesticated it, adopted some of its songs: and that is about all. Should we not ask God's Holy Spirit to flood our church life? Should we not give ourselves to serious intercession, for nights on end, and for a couple of days before our Synods? Should we not give massively for the extension of God's work rather than the tiny proportion we contribute at present – compared with the vast amount we spend on ourselves? Have we learned the basic lessons of surrender, prayer, self-denial, dependence on God's Spirit and passionate outreach? Should we not learn from our Asian friends that God pays for what he orders, and spend serious time seeking his face for what he does indeed order, at local and national church levels? Have we learnt to abjure the prerogatives of power and cultivate humility and self-sacrifice? Is this not what Christianity is all about?

Let us not imagine that this would militate against the variety of churchmanship which we celebrate in Western lands. That need not be so. These spiritual gifts are to be found in the largely Anglo-Catholic Diocese of Kuching just as they are in the largely evangelical Diocese of Singapore. It is not a question of churchmanship, but of obedience, of opening ourselves up to what God wants to give us and do through us, and put ourselves without reserve at his disposal. It is a matter of abiding in Christ like branches in the vine, and then allowing the sap of the vine to produce what fruit it will. No doubt some of the manifestations of that Spirit will be different in the West from what they are in the East, but they will bear the same marks of the Holy Spirit's activity. For as the apostle Paul put it so succinctly, 'The Spirit gives life', and we in the West are in danger of dying for lack of intimate, costly dependence on that same life-giving Spirit of God. Let us pray we will have the humility to learn from our brothers and sisters in South East Asia.

7

Learning from an
Asian Archdeacon

An archdeacon in the West is a senior church officer, working closely with the bishop of a diocese. He shares some of the bishop's oversight of clergy, but his main task is to see that the clergy are carrying out their duties and that the church property is in good order. In Sabah I found that those duties remain the same, but that a vigorous archdeacon has a far wider and more dynamic role. I think it would be instructive to record an interview I had with Archdeacon Fred David in February 2000, when I was attending the installation of the Rt Revd Datuk Yong Ping Chung as Archbishop of the Province of South East Asia, in succession to Archbishop Moses Tay. I should explain that despite his English-sounding name and his fluency in the English language, Fred David has an Indian father and a mixed Malaysian parentage on his mother's side: there is not a drop of English blood in his veins. He has for some years been a distinguished church leader in the interior of Borneo, notable for his evangelistic effectiveness and church-building skills. For the last couple of years he has been made Archdeacon of the Rural Interior. The interview was taped and ran like this:

MG You have been a pioneer evangelist in the interior for 16 years. What motivates you?

FD I remember once seeing a Chinese funeral. Gongs were sounded and a portrait of the dead man was carried in front of the funeral procession. It moved me to tears to think of this man going to the grave without knowing

Jesus Christ. I realized that in the Chinese community many others would be in that situation too. This profoundly challenged me to spread the gospel.

MG   Your diocese was born in mission. Do you think it is important to continue to major on evangelism?

FD   It is only through evangelism that the church can grow. The emphasis our diocese places on evangelism might seem a trifle aggressive, but I think our people then begin to see that each one of us has a part to play in bringing someone into the kingdom of God. Evangelism breeds excitement among churchpeople. For example, I have just led a Muslim to the Lord. He has been baptized and is being prepared for confirmation. As well as praying for people to discover the Lord, we must all be ready to evangelize.

MG   You mentioned evangelizing a Muslim. That is very unusual in the West. What led to the change in his life?

FD   He mentioned two things to me. He said he found Christianity very attractive in the fellowship and support it offered, support far greater than he had ever experienced with his Muslim friends. Second, it gave him assurance of eternal life. He had been very concerned about what would happen to him after death.

MG   But surely evangelizing Muslims is a highly sensitive matter?

FD   It is indeed, and the bishop has issued guidelines on the matter. The law in Sabah requires papers to be filled in, to show that conversion is in no way coerced. So I always hold public baptisms in the villages. I ask the village headman to have witnesses present. I ask the candidate if anyone is forcing him to be baptized. He answers 'No'. I then ask him if he truly desires to become a Christian. He says 'Yes'. I ask him if he believes in Jesus Christ and trusts him for a new life. Again he answers 'Yes'. I then turn to the headman and his colleagues and say, 'You have heard this man ask for baptism. Nobody has pressurized him. Will you give me permission to baptize him in the name of the Father and of the Son and of the Holy Spirit?' The headman agrees, and I say to the church, 'I am now going to proceed to baptize him into this faith God has given us.'

MG   Your country like mine is multi-faith. What right have you to promote Christianity, when people adhere to many other faiths?

FD   Well, we strongly believe that, as Acts 4.12 puts it, 'salvation is found in no-one else, for there is no other name under heaven given to men by which we must be saved'. It may sound arrogant, but Jesus is all we can offer people. The Church may not be able to offer money, as a lot of other religions in these parts are doing, presenting large cheques to new adherents. But we can offer peace in this life and eternal life beyond it. How could we keep silent?

MG   Is personal conversion important in church life here?

FD   Sure. I believe we need to bring a person to real conversion. Many people I meet in my ministry tell me that on a certain date their lives changed because they accepted Jesus Christ as Lord and Saviour.

MG   Witch doctors retain much power in your part of the world. Do you ever see conversions among them?

FD   I recall a witch doctor who was adamantly opposed to Christianity. I had been trying without success to point him to Christ. Then one day he had a dream, of his body floating in water. He came running to tell me. I asked him what he thought it meant. 'It means I am going to die. Please lead me to Christ. Show me how I can become a follower of his.' The man became a Christian and at Pentecost he brought all his charms and we burnt them. He remains alive and well!

Or I think of an old bedridden lady who was very sick and called in the witch doctors. They were unable to help. It so happened that we had a celebration in that village. She asked me and a colleague to come and pray for her. After the time of prayer she got up, began to walk and asked for food. She has now become a Christian but has, of course, incurred a great deal of opposition from the witch doctors.

MG Do you ever see whole communities coming to Christ in the jungle, as they seem to have done in the early church?

FD We frequently see the conversion of households. But here is an example of a whole village coming to Christ. In my travels I often pass a village where the inhabitants were reputed to be militant Muslims. One day my car had a puncture near the village. I was sweating copiously as I changed the tyre, and much to my surprise a man from the village invited me home for a drink. In his house I was amazed to sees a picture of Jesus. I said, 'I thought this village was Muslim. Where did you get this picture of Jesus?' He said, 'We do not believe in anything. As for the picture, I was given it ages ago, and I have been waiting for someone to explain to me about Jesus Christ.' And so I took the opportunity, and in due course the man became a Christian. And at Easter that year 48 of the village people including his children, grandchildren and in-laws all became Christians and I baptized them in the river. I believe households and whole villages can come to the Lord because the Lord longs to save them.

MG How do you manage to combine the role of an archdeacon with that of pastor, evangelist and pioneer?

FD When the bishop asked me to be an archdeacon, I agreed so long as it would not hinder me from what I am doing. He was happy for that. Consequently, being an archdeacon is secondary. My primary vocation is to see people come to the Lord, nurture them, and release them into ministry. The bishop is now revising the role of archdeacon. It is to be one of motivating and equipping people within the church.

MG I was struck, reading the Diocesan Report, that you are doing leadership training. In my country that would be an unusual role for an archdeacon. Have you any advice for us?

FD   Three things come to mind. First, there must be a clear vision: what has God called us to do? Once we have that vision clear, we can go ahead and address it. Second, we need to get our hearts right. For example, God has called me to be a pastor and an evangelist, and these things must have priority in my ministry. Third, we need to get the church moving. This requires leaders who can train lay people in leadership. And we need to move away from the fear that they will take over our job! I look to Ephesians 4.11 and see a vision of prophets, evangelists, pastors and teachers – a team supporting and supplementing one another in the mission of the church. In recent years we have seen this teamwork growing, and the result is fresh churchplanting.

MG   You mentioned prophets just now. Do you find that to be a current gift in your churches?

FD   Yes. We find that we are given a 'word of knowledge' sometimes about some new situation into which a church member is going. Neither I nor my colleagues have any human knowledge of the situation, but under the guidance of God's Holy Spirit we may be able to speak something very helpful and sometimes predictive into that situation. The person is immediately aware of the reality and truth of what we are saying.

MG   I am very struck that here in South East Asia the proclamation of the gospel and the 'signs following' go closely together, as in the New Testament. Do you see healing and exorcism in your work?

FD   Yes. As a matter of fact only a couple of days ago I was called out at midnight for deliverance ministry, for the second time this week. When people come out of native religions into the church, it is not surprising that they can be seriously disturbed by influences from their past and ask us to help them. They do not go to the shaman or medicine man any more. That, of course, is to invite trouble. So they come to us for help. We pray for wisdom to discern whether their condition is psychological or demonic.

MG   Could you explain what you do in a deliverance ministry?

FD   When there is sickness or evidence of evil spirits, I always minister with a team of three or four Christian colleagues. I talk to the family and find out the background to the problem. In particular I am keen to know whether there are particular times when the person is manifesting these symptoms. This may help us discern whether the problem is psychological, emotional or demonic. We then move into a time of worship, and I believe this is crucial. In the course of it God often shows us the way we should proceed to deal with the case. We are very dependent on the guidance of God's Spirit, because cases can be very different. If we need more time for fasting and prayer before moving into ministry we will take it. But often we are able to minister at once, and see the Lord setting the person free. We will then counsel the patient, seek to bring him to a deeper reliance on Christ, and pray for him to be filled with the Holy Spirit.

MG   I am struck, in glancing at your material, that every church in your diocese has to respond annually to four questions: their greatest breakthrough, their biggest problem, their forthcoming plans and their prayer needs. That seems unusually well defined, to Western eyes. Do you feel that clear goals like that are important?

FD   Clear goals are vital. So is their implementation. That is a major part of my work as archdeacon. I visit the churches in my area and evaluate them in the light of those four areas. The top leadership in the diocese is very keen to see the church double in attendance, and in order to achieve that clear goals and careful monitoring is essential. We want to leave a church that is dynamic for the generations to come.

MG How do you nurture new Christians, when many of them come straight out of paganism?

FD I believe in a fairly brief period before baptism, because the candidates are subject to a lot of political and social pressure until they are baptized. But after that the pressure diminishes. This gives me space to give a much longer time to preparing the candidates for confirmation. We take three years! In the first year we concentrate on discipleship. In the second year I want to help them grow into ministry. By the third year I want to see them taking practical steps in ministry and beginning to exercise leadership. So at the time of their confirmation by the bishop, we always send these people out in mission teams to the villages. In this way we give them hands-on experience of what their responsibilities are as adult Christians within the Church. Every Christian is meant to have a ministry, and so I try to help them discover what that ministry is and equip them for it.

More generally, I believe that nurture is an ongoing affair, best achieved through practical ministry. So I always have new Christians coming out with me into the villages and sharing, to a small degree, in the teaching. We find that when a person bears testimony to the difference Christ has made in his own life, it is very effective.

MG Going beyond nurture, how do you train your leaders?

FD Training demands sacrifice, particularly the sacrifice of time. My family is very understanding about this, knowing that it is for the sake of the Kingdom of God. But it is certainly demanding. It really means sharing our lives with the potential leader. I try to transfer to them what God has shared with me. In this way, multiplication takes place. That is the aim.

In practice, we are having four main leadership training periods this year, putting people into training modules. We want to equip them, so that they can go into the villages and train others also: in evangelism, the use of Scripture, discipleship and nurturing.

MG I believe that, like us in the West, you have a big problem with youth. You could easily lose a whole generation. How are you handling this?

FD We need to take a fresh look at work with young people. Even in the jungle they are influenced by the worldwide web, and are heavily into computers! As you know, youth work is not easy. But we have made a start.

In the last two years we have run a number of youth festivals. Every two months we get the young people of the churches together. Only last week we had one such festival with 300 young people gathering. There was Christian disco music and dimmed lights, dancing, and fun. Instead of preaching I used dialogue. We had a Christian doctor, teacher and policeman with us. I began to ask them questions about AIDS, school drop-outs and drugs. We tried to apply God's principles to these very live issues, and by the end of the seminar the young people understood that the Lord wants their bodies as temples for his Holy Spirit, and this calls for purity of life. At that festival 25 young people committed their lives to Christ, after pondering the challenge presented to them. By the end of the year we expect some 300 young people to become Christians. We must make a conscious effort to understand and win our young people. Let's grow with the times, and respond to the way they talk and the way they dress. They are saying something to us.

MG Fred, you are a dynamic leader. Many people in charge of churches are not. Have you a word for them?

FD Don't despair. Many leadership skills can be learnt. But we need to have a teachable heart. If someone is doing something better elsewhere, have the humility to go and learn from him. And *desire* is so important. Every pastor needs to cultivate a deep desire to see his church grow both in depth and numbers. That should stimulate him to want to learn the best available ways of leadership.

MG   Fred, have you a word for us in the West?

FD   I am glad to be an Anglican. I will always be an Anglican, and I treasure my roots. But I think that we Anglicans need to have a paradigm shift and return to the Word of God. We seem to have rather lost that perspective. Missionaries who came from England brought the Word of God to us, and the church in Asia has been built on that Word. We all need to continue to build on that foundation.

It is very difficult for archdeacons in England. They are dealing all the time with ancient churches and shortage of finance. But when that has been taken into account, as it must, I fancy our Western church leaders could learn something from an archdeacon like that!

8

Just Learning

———•—

I think I have detected for some time a reluctance in the Western church to learn from the East. We do not call them 'mission churches' any more, and we take pains to be politically correct. But all the same we feel, deep down, just a little superior. We certainly do not tend to emulate them very much. This is particularly the case in the area of mission and evangelism. We are well aware how fast the gospel is growing in places like Nigeria and Singapore, and yet we persuade ourselves that it must be easier for them, or that the climate is more conducive, or... And we do not take on board the lessons which their fruitfulness has to teach what is all too often our fruitlessness. I have had the privilege of seeing a good deal of the work of this young Province, and I am convinced it has much to teach us.

We desperately need to learn from them. I write in March 2000, when the Church of England Synod has just received a damning survey among churchpeople and non-churchgoers, commissioned by the Archbishops' Council and carried through by Ms Jane Ozanne. It saw clergy as 'grey men in suits, often in ivory towers'. The church 'tries to look trendy, but it's only skin deep. It seems like a club – only for those on the inside'. Indeed, it was seen as 'isolated from the rest of society'. Vestments and robes constitute a major barrier. Bishops try 'to be all things to all men' and the only bishop who stood out was James Jones of Liverpool. As for young people, only one group of them could be assembled for this survey because of the massive disinterest of young people in the Church and all it stands for. Among the under-25s the only Christian role model they could name was Sir Cliff Richard, but the general response was, 'There isn't one. They are all middle-class old men with white hair and no dress sense.'

Who can say that against the background of such strictures, the church in the West has nothing to learn from Asia?

When Bishop Chiu Ban It became the first Asian bishop of Singapore in 1966, and later under the leadership of Bishop Moses Tay, the situation for the Anglican Church was just as problematic as it currently is for the church in the West. They faced an industrial, multi-faith society, ignorant of the Christian faith and indifferent to its claims. Their leaders found themselves called to preside over a church which was very Western and rather effete. It had certainly made little advance in many years. But their emphasis on commitment to evangelism, prayer and fasting, fearless proclamation of biblical Christianity, careful congregational training, youth work, and dependence on the power of the Holy Spirit, his gifts as well as his graces – all this has transformed the situation. Their remarkable emphasis on love in action has opened many avenues for the gospel in this province. The sheer generosity and self-sacrifice of the Christians has not gone unnoticed. It is very attractive, but very costly. They have been prepared to pay the price. 'Love Malaysia' and 'Love Singapore' has not just been a motto but a way of life. Sadly, in the West, loving social action and enthusiastic proclamation of the gospel have, until comparatively recently, been espoused by different wings of the Anglican Church. The more liberal Christians have been great on Christian action but rather weak on Christian proclamation. The more evangelical Christians have tended to be strong on the proclamation and weaker on the practical manifestations of that love which demonstrates the life of heaven on earth. The combination of the two is a lesson for all to see in the spread of the gospel in South East Asia.

The cell church has prove an invaluable way of making new Christians and of building up lay witness and fellowship. It is not the only way in which Christian advance can take place, but it is a highly effective way. Indeed, most great movements in the world, both religious and secular, have advanced through their cell structure: the Communists are a good case in point. To be sure, it may be questioned whether the cell structure is authentically Anglican. Much of the most fruitful life in Anglican Christianity has emerged from below while the cell churches tend often to be controlled from the top. But when you see successful examples of this movement, in Singapore, Sabah or somewhere in England like Thame, it is evident that there need be no conflict between a church based on cells and authentic Anglicanism. The cell church may indeed point a way ahead for us. It is so vibrant and vigorous, whereas all the indications are that our traditional structures are in poor shape. Many of our ordinands are looking in the direction of the cell church. We might be unwise to turn our backs on this proven method of Christian advance.

Churchplanting is not something we have done much of in Britain, though it is beginning to happen nowadays. Our forefathers in the past thousand years have done it for us! But the Christians in the Far East have extensive current experience of it, and a passion to make it happen. It is possible to found a new church with only a handful of committed members, meeting initially in a home. It can take off from there. Of course the transition to the churchplanting mindset and the churchplanting cell is not easy. It involves trusting and training lay leaders. It involves the parent church losing members and providing support, finance and oversight in the early days of the plant. It involves saying farewell to ecclesiastical buildings and accoutrements, in most cases, and forming an informal and people-friendly church. But is that not something that we badly need in Britain, where many a parish church is in the wrong place and many of our housing estates utterly devoid of any church presence at all? The cell church is so flexible, and can easily be moved if its members change location. It is so accessible and non-threatening to those who find a traditional church such a hazard. If we are wondering how to bridge the gap between the church and society, surely this is a way worth trying?

Then again, the area of leadership is one where we have

much to learn. The British style is rather laid back and for the most part non-directive. That may not be a bad thing. But the clear goals which the Asian churches espouse, the thorough oversight, and the reporting to bishop and synod each year on their vision for the parish, their greatest breakthrough, their greatest plans and their greatest prayer needs is surely one which we could profitably adopt. Equally it would be good if church leadership at parish, diocesan and national level was rather more fearless about acknowledging Jesus Christ and inviting others to him. Many people in our land do not know what the church stands for. In South East Asia they are left in little doubt. As I move around our country I sense much sorrow among churchpeople that the trumpet sound from our leaders is often so muted.

As for the work of the Holy Spirit, what can one say? There is no doubt that a major spiritual movement is encompassing South East Asia, whereas the climate in England remains spiritually frigid. Human beings cannot change that. It is no good urging people to employ spiritual gifts which are alien to them. We need a profound drenching by the gracious waters of the Spirit. But there is something we can do. When we are aware of those gifts in our midst, we can use them without embarrassment. When we know full well that we lack spiritual power we can implore the Lord for it. Did not Jesus say, 'If you, being evil, know how to give good gifts to your children, how much more will your heavenly Father give the Holy Spirit to those who ask him?'

Finally, if church leaders would reflect on my interview with the archdeacon in the previous chapter, and see how his priorities and approaches matched their own, I cannot doubt that this would be both challenging and beneficial.

Just as parents need to learn from their children when they are grown up, so Western churches need to learn from their spiritual children now that they have grown to such a stature. We in the West need to retain our L plates!